Recommendations of Eminent Personalities

I am surprised to see this book, 'Indian Film Music and The Aesthetics of Chords'. The author has picked an unusual subject in the context of Indian music scenario. I would like to congratulate and send best wishes to the author for this great work.

Burjor Lord
(Veteran Indian film musician)

Till date, a lot of ink has been utilised to discover the magic, mystery, and mastery of music. However, very few books from India have managed to capture the very essence about the aesthetics of chords. Abhishek Tripathi's book is a window to this valuable information covering all aspects of music like chords, melody, tune making, orchestration, and its aesthetics. The book's uniqueness reflects Abhishek's deep passion and knowledge of music. In this new age music, this book is a breath of fresh air for all aspiring and professional musicians.

Ashok Jagtap
(Violin maestro;
former Cine Musicians Association president)

I want to congratulate Dr. Abhishek Tripathi that he has written this book on the aesthetics of chords which reveals how to use chords and theories in music.

Sunil Kaushik
(Senior Guitarist of Indian Cinema)

I feel 'Indian Film Music and The Aesthetics of Chords' is a very informative book. It will be beneficial for the students of music, and budding composers and arrangers.

Pt. Bhavdeep Jaipurwale
(Music composer, arranger and teacher)

Abhishek Tripathi has truly given us a Holistic view on how Chords of music and its Technique can help create a unique Sound of Music! Truly well written, showcasing the Psychological, Physical and Spiritual aura of twelve notes of Music.

Merlin D'souza
(Pianist and Composer)

Indian Film Music and The Aesthetics of Chords

Decoding the thoughts of a composer

Abhishek Tripathi

ZORBA BOOKS

ZORBA BOOKS

Publishing Services by Zorba Books, August 2020

Website: www.zorbabooks.com
Email: info@zorbabooks.com
Contact: 0124-4259579/8800509579

Cover design by Sithesh

Copyright © Abhishek Tripathi

ISBN Print Book - 978-93-90011-47-6
ISBN eBook - 978-93-90011-48-3

All rights reserved. No part of this book may be reproduced or transmitted in any form or by any means, electronic or mechanical, except by a reviewer. The reviewer may quote brief passages, with attribution, in a review to be printed in a magazine, newspaper, or on the Web—without permission in writing from the copyright owner.

The publisher under the guidance and direction of the author has published the contents in this book, and the publisher takes no responsibility for the contents, it's accuracy, completeness, any inconsistencies, or the statements made. The contents of the book do not reflect the opinion of the publisher or the editor. The publisher and editor shall not be liable for any errors, omissions, or the reliability of the contents of the book.

Any perceived slight against any person/s, place or organization is purely unintentional.

Zorba Books Pvt. Ltd. (opc)
Sushant Arcade,
Next to Courtyard Marriot,
Sushant Lok 1, Gurgaon – 122009, India

*I dedicate this book to
My Mummy and Papa*

I am proud to be a part of their lives.

TABLE OF CONTENTS

Acknowledgements .... *ix*
Foreword .... *xi*
Preface .... *xiii*
A Starstruck Afternoon .... *xix*
(An exclusive meeting with
legendary music composer Pyarelal Sharma)

Chapter 1
Introduction 1
    Aesthetics, Chords, Aesthetics of Chords, Orchestration, Indian Film Music, Aesthetics of Music, Tune/Melody, Tune Making

Chapter 2
Chords 15
    Principles and Theories of Chord Formation
    Sound Physics of Notes and Chord, Theories about Interval Ratio, Resonance, Wavelength and Oscillation, Types of Chords and its Classification, More on Chord Progression, Aesthetics of Chords- Perceptions, Hypothesis, Theories and Views about Moods, Usage of Chords and Harmony in Indian Film Music
    Study of Chords and its Aesthetics in Compositions and Orchestration of Prominent Indian Film Composers

Chapter 3
Tune Making and Aesthetics 61
    What is a Tune, Perfect Tune, Types of Tunes and Musical Structures, Thought Process of Making a Tune - Perception Building, Making a Theme,

Developing the Theme to a Musical Structure, Reaching on a Perfect Tune, Testing for Acceptance, Presentation Design of a Tune, Views and Critics on the Tune Making Process and Music Production, Do's & Don'ts in Tune Making, Tune Making in India, Impact of Knowledge of Chords in Making and Developing a Tune, Indian Raga System vs. Chord Progression System in Tune Making, Impact of Knowledge and Education in Tune Making, Aesthetics of Chords in Tune Making, Effects of Aesthetics of Composer on Tune- Own Aesthetics and Borrowed Aesthetics (Inspiration)

Chapter 4

Orchestration 111

Defining Orchestra and Orchestration, Sangat or Accompaniment vs. Orchestration (Soloism vs. Groupism), Principles of Orchestration- Sections of Musical Instruments & Vocals, Writing for Different Segments for a Tune's Expression, Aesthetics of Chords in Making Orchestra of a Tune

Chapter 5

Aesthetics of Composer
in Perceptual Process of a Tune 133

Cultural, Social, Economic Background and Learning of Composer, Sound Physics Factors, Psychological Factors, Ethnicity, Social and Economic Factors

Chapter 6

Aesthetics of Chords in Indian Film Music 149

Conclusive Statements on Aesthetics of Indian Film Music regarding Chords and Orchestrations

Bibliography 159

Acknowledgements

I would like to thank my research guide and supervisor Dr. Akhilesh Sapre for his valuable guidance and time. Being a maestro of Indian Classical instrument Sitar, he provided useful tips and demonstrations related to the beauty of melody and music, which will remain a lifetime treasure for me.

I seek the blessing of my guruji, former All India Radio music composer Late Pandit Jwala Prasad, who left us for heavenly abode in 2019. He has always played a huge influence on my creativity and his compositions continue to inspire me every single day.

Veteran Bollywood music arranger Late Shri Kersi Lord gave me an overview regarding the harmonies and their use in films. He also shared his experience of the working culture of the film industry, when I met him for an interview. I am very grateful to him.

Amar Haldipur, a very close companion of the dynamic legendary composer duo Laxmikant-Pyarelal for over decades, has always been a great inspiration for me. From 2004 till now, he has guided me and given several tips on composing film music. He has shared with me minute observations regarding the working of Laxmikant-Pyarelal, iconic singer Lata Mangeshkar, among many other musicians, while passing on the learning from his own experiences. He has had a great impression on me and helped me shape knowledge of music. I feel immense pleasure to thank him and salute his musical work.

In continuation, I am grateful towards the support I got from eminent musicians like Burjor Lord, Ashok Jagtap, Kishore

Sharma, Sunil Kaushik, Pt. Bhavdeep Jaipurwale, Merlin Desouza, Sharda Rajan, and Shridhar Nagraj as their valuable inputs for this work. I also thank Mr. Sudarshan Pandey for his support.

I would also like to thank my friends for their incredible support. My parents Mrs. Shanti and Mr. Sevaram Tripathi, who encouraged me to pursue this research, have always been a boon for my creations. I am proud to get their blessings. My eldest brother Dr. Ashish Tripathi supported me creatively, alongwith Neelam *bhabhi*. My elder brother Manish Tripathi, and Nandani *bhabhi* also always encouraged me for my work. Sakhi, Sabad, Shaurya, Samyak and Shreshtha—the kids of our unique home—ensured that I stayed energised throughout the journey.

Tara, my soulmate, who is also a great singer, has remained a constant source of strength and support. She guided me while looking after our son Samyak (Raagi) and managing her busy schedule. I feel proud to have such a wonderful life partner and would like to thank her with all my heart.

While preparing the final draft, I am glad to have had helping hands like Mr. Rahul Sharma and Mr. Dinesh Bajpai. The editing process became easy because of Ms. Yael Ajgarni, who gave my work the perfect finishing touch.

Foreword

*D*r. Abhishek Tripathi's 'Indian Film Music and The Aesthetics of Chords' is an excellent book with easy-to-read, quality information on the subject. For those in the music industry, having the knowledge of chords is extremely important. I feel that even coming up with the idea of writing on this subject is a big deal. Chords are highly valued and popular among musicians across the globe as they provide the necessary base for compositions. In Indian music, the tanpura is typically tuned to Sa and Pa. This is also chord, and harmony. It provides a base to the performer and helps in creating an ambience.

Through this book, Tripathi has made several factual arguments in relation to chords. He has called a chord "the smallest kind of composition". "Like how sentences comprise words, a harmony or a chord progression is made up of chords," he has said in the book.

Over the years, the world has witnessed many experimentations in music arrangements. Those who possessed enough knowledge and had greater understanding of chords were successful in creating good arrangements in the past. Legendary musician Pyarelal Sharma is known for his wonders in arranging music. He would create one melody on one instrument, have five to six chord variations after that melody and then come back to the main chord. His creations were truly inspirational. One of his best works was seen in 'Main To Ek Khwaab Hun' from the film Himalaya Ki God Mein, rendered by Mukesh and composed by Kalyanji Anandji. If you carefully hear the second interlude of this song, you will understand what chords are all about. Pay attention to the french horn and the chords backing the main melody on the horn.

In this book, Tripathi has discussed important topics in detail. He has given such insights of the film music industry that one can only talk about after deep thinking and contemplation. His writing shows he has a profound understanding of chords. His knowledge is backed by his experiences as a composer and research on the subject. In my entire career in the film industry, I have rarely come across people like Tripathi who know so much about chords.

I feel extremely happy to know that this book will now be available to readers. I believe that this book will not only be useful to musicians, aspirant composers and students but also be loved by general music lovers. This book will also help open new dimensions towards understanding the aesthetics of chords.

Kishore Sharma
(Music Composer and Arranger)

Preface

The process of making a music composition or a song just from lyrics is a work of art. Different skills are used for the artistic result, and an artist's individual experience plays a key role in shaping his aesthetics. For a composer, the biggest factor in making a tune is his individuality. The development of aesthetics depends upon acquired skills and knowledge, experience and sensitivity of a person, and that's why aesthetics of every person is different. Culture, society, economy, psychological surroundings are other factors that affect the aesthetics of a person.

I got inclined toward composing music in my early childhood. I feel that my aesthetics gradually developed by hearing many popular songs several times, as I analysed tunes, orchestration, songs and singing styles. As I became more passionate about the songs, I found myself craving for more knowledge. It was a point when I got into self exploration. Later, my focus shifted to the chords. It was a little difficult and a slower process for me because I hail from an Indian music background and there is no significance of chords in classical music. Chords are mainly used in light and film music in India.

It is quite interesting to think about quarter tones, also known as 'qt'. The 12-tone tempered scale is the most common tuning system, but Turkish, Arabic and Persian music is based on quarter tone scales which involves 24 equal tones in an octave, that's why their music sounds different from the rest. The Middle East invented this 24-tone equal temperament, also known as 24-TET, and these musical thoughts were proposed by Heinrich Richer (in 1823) and Mikhail Mishaqah (around 1840).

The Middle East has different aesthetics when it comes to tonal interpretations and it certainly sounds unique and interesting. I heard Bayati scale and its *maqam* (musical mode), and it is as beautiful as the Indian *raga* Bhairavi and as soulful as the Indian classical music. What we hear as Azaan — the Islamic call to prayer — in different mosques, from my presumption, is based on the Bayati scale.

The Bayati scale has all notes of Indian Raga Bhairavi but the second note is located between Komal Re (flat second) and Shuddh Re (perfect second). This difference adds to its uniqueness in reference to Indian music, and so it makes a variation in the aesthetic senses of a listener. Music of the Middle East is very similar to Indian music in terms of movements and structures, and hence, many music composers from India find inspiration in the eastern music.

The most famous Bayati composition '*Al Balad Al Mehboob*' was used by the famous music composer duo Shankar-Jaikishan in the 1951 film '*Awara*' for the song '*Ghar Aaya Mera Pardesi*'. The composition's popularity even today shows the audience's great affinity with foreign scales and the composers were also very keen to compose it to be remembered. Another Arabian scale, Maqam Kurd, also has notes similar to the Indian *raga* Bhairavi and it is used as frequently in the Middle East as Bhairavi is used in India. The same case is with ancient Indian classical music where all music was based on 22 microtones, called *shrutis*, stretched in an octave. One important example of microtone between two semitones is in raga Darbari, where *komal gandhar* (flat 3rd) is further flattened with almost one microtone. These are the elements of music which also contributes to the aesthetics of composers and listeners, of course a choice-based phenomenon of different origins and ethnicities.

Cadence — another beautiful element, which can also be called as musical punctuation — is associated with aesthetics. They are meant to serve as phrases for harmonic resolutions of a certain part of melody or harmony. A perfect cadence resolves the harmony from 5th degree to the 1st degree. A plagal cadence is a little different, where the 4th degree gets resolved into the 1st degree. Perfect and plagal cadences give the final resolution to the harmonic movement because both end on the 1st degree of scale i.e. tonic (the tonal center of harmony). When harmony goes to 5th degree from any other degree, it is called half cadence and it needs further to be resolved. Like perfect cadence, imperfect cadence is a movement but it doesn't have the chord in their root positions. A deceptive cadence is a false cadence which results in dominant harmony i.e., 5th degree into any of the other degrees, particularly excluding 1st degree only.

Apart from using perfect and plagal cadences, an intelligent use of half or deceptive cadence may create more harmonic adventure, in lieu of common progressions. Specially deceptive cadences can be very useful and sound unusual too otherwise, because here, an anticipated progression does not come to the expected degree and it may fall on 6th or 4th (either in their plain or variants like 7th, 6th, augmented, diminished or whatsoever), which creates harmonic tension again to be resolved further.

Negative harmony is one of the most powerful tools for developing aesthetics of chords because it gives some good options for adding extra and fancy sound to the main progression and sometimes these options may become a part of basic progression, too. Some creative changes to the melody also may be obtained through this tool. It was propagated by Ernst Levy, a Swiss musician. In negative harmony, every major chord gets converted into some minor chord and vise versa. Other chords like 7th, 6th or with more complex harmonies, also get converted to another form, so it is very useful when you are in search of a different chord or melody to add on extra colours to the musical structure. The transformation of notes is proposed as interchangeables like; C-G, D♭-G♭, D-F, E♭-E, B♭-A, A♭-B. Practising negative harmony as a tool will certainly add some more colours to the music.

Modal interchange also allows one to access more options for changing the harmonies. In modal interchange, the chords are replaced by the same degree of any other modal scale from the same tonal center. For instance, if one is working on C Ionian and the tonic is Cmaj7, so the 6th chord will be Am7, and if we replace this chord with the same degree of C Phrygian i.e., A♭ maj7 will come in the place of C Ionian i.e., Am7. This is called modal interchange. It helps to get different sounds together at a certain place of chord progression or melody. Modal interchange can be used according to the aesthetic need and one's satisfaction.

To use modal interchange and other tools to get the optional harmonies, one should have proper knowledge of scales, degrees and modes. In Indian music, there are many classical *ragas* which share similarities with some foreign scales. Pentatonic scale has similarity with Indian *raga* Bhupali. Kumoi pentatonic scale is also very similar to the raga Shivranjani. Double harmonic minor scale involves flat 2nd, perfect 3rd, perfect 4th, perfect 5th, flat 6th and a perfect 7th; it is just similar to the Indian raga Bhairav. Hence, a deep knowledge of Indian classical music and foreign scales will certainly be useful to develop the ears and the consonance and dissonance may pave way for better aesthetics.

Stacked notes in a particular manner in any melodic progression also bring an innovative touch to the melodic and harmonic structures of a composer. Renowned composer Arnold Shoenberg, in his composition Chamber Symphony No.1 Op.9, beautifully used the stacked 4th. Chromatic alterations are also very useful in the process of aesthetic development of a composer and may add on in the compositions very creatively and beautifully. Changing of the key center will also be aesthetically useful, if done wisely.

Sometimes, using polytonality of chords with triple pedal points helps create new sound and aesthetics to the musical structure. Pedal point is a point where one or more notes are sustained and another melody or sound may move by a different progression of chords. It typically works with bass or double bass tones and it functions as a non-chord tone while the progression of chords goes in another direction. However, sometimes it is used with higher octave notes, and then it is called an inverted pedal point. It helps develop the relation of consonant and dissonant sounds until the harmony reaches its final resolution.

Learning is an endless process. Since I have been in this process for a long time, constant self exploration has given me a strong will to study about chords and their aesthetics and pushed me to contribute to research. The topic 'Aesthetics of Chords in Tune Making and Orchestration: In Subjective Context of Indian Film Music' was of keen interest to me. The day I started working on it, I was aware that my work will only be a drop in the ocean, but I still hope it will at least open a new window for learners and researchers. This book is a result of this research. However, some changes and additions were also made to make it more interesting.

Lastly, this book would not have been possible without the contributions of my well-wishers and a few great personalities. I want to salute and thank them. I hope this book paves way for new discussions regarding the aesthetics of chords.

Abhishek Tripathi

Email : abhishekpurchase@gmail.com
Facebook : https://www.facebook.com/abhishektripathimusic/
Twitter : @DrAbhishekTrip8
LinkedIn : https://www.linkedin.com/in/dr-abhishek-tripathi-9a250a53

A Starstruck Afternoon

*(An exclusive meeting with
legendary music composer Pyarelal Sharma)*

On a cloudy afternoon in Mumbai, I rang the doorbell, which a graceful old lady answered. She invited me in when I saw a man, fully dressed in white, appear from behind her. Oh my god! Was this a dream, I asked myself. This man was a living legend, the master of Indian film music who had a tremendous fan following; I had heard many of his songs on the radio during my childhood, and I had recently watched a performance online of his symphony in Germany.

He was a legend whose compositions were said to be at par with the gods of music like Mozart and Beethoven. My mind was all over the place and I almost felt my vision blur up because of the overpowering white attire. Overwhelmed by feelings of love, respect and devotion, I reached out and touched his feet. This was Shri Pyarelal Sharma, one of the epitomes of Indian film music, and the lady who had welcomed me into their home was his wife Sunila ji, whom I addressed as Mata ji (an exhortation for mother in Hindi). Both of them greeted me with their inviting smiles.

As he began speaking, he had several questions regarding my book and knowledge. I could feel him testing me in his unique way, but I was nervous and mostly stayed mum at the beginning of the conversation. It took me a while, almost an hour, to get comfortable with him.

I got the privilege of having a cup of tea and some snacks with the music legend, which further helped me ease into the surrounding. Answering one of my queries, he said, "You are writing a book on aesthetics of chords. It is good. You came to meet me; it shows that you are very passionate about your work. I wish to work on a national level for the education of composers and musicians. For that, I will need at least twelve good teachers who know everything. Music is my life. I wish that the new generation comes forward for the work. We have plenty of talent."

He added that though western artists knew everything about their music, they also tend to be envious of Indians because of their music. "But if you have adequate knowledge of western music, they (western musicians) will give proper response and priority to your work. Indian music is far ahead of others but there are many things yet to be achieved, while western music is complete in itself. I started reading good books in 1950. They helped me a lot. My father only taught me for about two months, rest I learnt everything on my own. I also learnt western music very keenly."

I was very excited to hear him speak about his experience. This drove me to ask him about music and the preparation needed to become a good composer. He opened up a little more and, to fulfil my curiosities, spoke on the importance of learning music and its technical points. He said, "A music composer should know all the things related to chords and its inversions, notes and scales. What is music arrangement? It is important to know about obbligato, notation and its system etc. Being a writer, you should be aware of everything. What are the types of clef and how to read them is a must to know. What are the sections of instruments, in which clef they are written and played, what it denotes, what is scoring, the technical details of film scoring, how the beats and bar are written, what the great composers had already written... you should know the answers to all these questions."

On the background scoring for films, he said, "In a scene, there are major and minor details, like a boy entering the frame, seeing a girl, the camera zooming on him, the start of the next shot, etc. You have to consider everything while composing for background as well as playback. Every composer writes in his own way. He uses scales and degrees according to his perceptions."

I was swimming deep in the ocean of profound knowledge being shared with me, as he emphasised on the utility and importance of my book. He showed me his collection of books, which he evidently treasured. "Books are very important; if you have to know about something specific, the books will definitely have the answers. A composer must know how to conduct and how to arrange things. Music has its dictionary. Unlike Indian music, western music is completely writable. You can write more than three hundred emotions there. So, whether you are writing a book or composing music, do it perfectly, because people see wrong or bad things first."

I was now trying to have a good look at his collection while being attentive. There were so many questions scrolling through my mind I was hesitant to ask much. After taking a deep breath, I mustered the courage to ask him about chords.

He replied, "There is *maqam* in Arabian music which is equivalent to *raga* in Indian music. We use Sa-Pa or Sa-Ma in *taanpura* when we sing Indian raga, and likewise, chords are used in western music. It is a complete system. If you are going to a party, you should wear a suit. The same thought applies in this case; if you are going for music, you should know the system of chords. Everyone has their own choice of chords. As you learn, the range of choices increases. Your knowledge of chords facilitates your way of thinking. There is no end. First, you have to make a habit of different harmonies and then it starts giving you pleasure and fun. When you are full of knowledge, even for a small filler music, you think a hundred times and you keep coming up with a new idea every time."

We were allotted only an hour for this meeting but it was already two hours by now. I ensured that I gained as much knowledge as I could. He then went on to talk about his work and new ventures. Despite being over 75 years of age, he spoke with so much energy and talked about writing for overseas musicians. With a feel of nostalgia, he said, "Except Shankar-Jaikishan and O.P. Nayyar, I worked with everyone. All of them have worked in their own way. Laxmikant ji was from Indian music and I was trained in western music… The work of music composition cannot be taught. It is how we don't fall in love intentionally, but naturally. I did my first music arrangement at the age of fourteen. It was for the film *'Phir Subah Hogi'* and the music director was Khayyam *sahab*. In 2016, I did a symphony in Germany. I wrote a quartet also, which is now being performed. Now, I am not only an Indian film composer. In a concert of repute, there were only three composers whose compositions were performed and they were Mozart, Beethoven and yours truly Pyarelal Sharma. So, music has so much work and lessons that you can't finish learning it completely even after in many births."

During the whole conversation, he used his piano many times to elaborate on his thoughts. I was thrilled to see his fingers, which travelled through the keys like a breeze. While elaborating on the chords and scales, he showed one of his earlier experiments done in the process of composition. With his fingers running on the piano, he said, "Have you heard the song *'Bandhan Toote Na Sanwariya'* from the film *'Mom Ki Gudiya'*? We used shuddh Re (perfect second note) prominently instead of komal Re (flat second note) of the base *raga* in the composition. According to our classical music, it was totally wrong but we did it as an experiment. We used changes like this for doing something different and new. This brought a sharper and developed mindset to our work."

At one point he became very emotional when he spoke about his music partner Laxmikant ji. He allowed me to see the old photographs on his wall, where some of the old memories were affixed as lifelong assets. These pictures were of music director R.D. Burman, Laxmikant ji and famous lyricist Anand Bakshi. "He (Laxmikant ji) had no ego, actually. In business, he was up to the mark. We met in 1952 and worked together till 1998. Our chemistry was so strong like a matching blood group. I feel his presence all the time when I speak to people. He was a tremendous human."

Pyarelal ji's work abroad made me wonder about his versatility. How were his learning and practices? I asked him about his initial days and the musicians who inspired him then.

He said, "I used to listen to Gary Goldsmith, John Williams and Dave Brubeck in my early days. My violin teacher was Mr. Anthony Gonsalves. He was a great artist. I was taught by him at the age of twelve. That time, I was working in Ranjeet Studio at Dadar area of Mumbai. My shift timing was 10 a.m. to 5 pm. I used to take a bus at 6:50 a.m. to go to Flora Fountain. From Flora Fountain to Colaba, I would walk to reach the place of Anthony sir where my timing was 8 to 9 a.m.. After that, I would go to BSO (Bombay Symphony Orchestra) and BCO (Bombay Chamber Orchestra) at that time and then catch a train for office at Dadar. Most of the time, I would be late to reach office but it was always overlooked because I was still a child. In the evening, I would attend classes at St. Michael Night School. I lived near Kirti College at that time."

It was a great pleasure to meet a legend like him. When the time came for me to leave, Pyarelal ji and his wife blessed me for my upcoming work and promised to meet me again soon. I left knowing that I had just had an encounter that I will cherish for the rest of my life.

Chapter 1

Introduction

"If you are going to a party, you should wear a suit. The same thought applies in this case; if you are going for music, you should know the system of chords. Everyone has their own choice of chords. As you learn, the range of choices increases. Your knowledge of chords facilitates your way of thinking. There is no end. First, you have to make a habit of different harmonies and then it starts giving you pleasure and fun. When you are full of knowledge, even for a small filler music, you think a hundred times and you keep coming up with a new idea every time."

-Pyarelal Sharma

AESTHETICS

What is beauty? It's not a question that has a specific answer. For some, beauty can be limited by following the set standards, while for others it can be limitless. It can be a qualitative thought or a hypothesis. You can work out the factors which make a thing or a thought beautiful. In music, it may be physical or imaginative, in reference to the audience or a composer. The value of beauty cannot be identified in quantitative measures, as Ramesh Kuntal Megh said, "Beauty is the subject of human assessment... It's a human state."[1]

Around 1735-50, a German philosopher, Baumgarten used the term 'aesthetics', to study beauty as a subject. Aesthetics is all about the aesthetic sense towards beauty, attraction, passion, etc. Baumgarten has seen philosophy in three different parts: logic, ethics, and aesthetics.

Beauty is a relative term and its impact differs from person to person. That's why a universal statement about beauty is impossible to make. Baumgarten propagated aesthetics as a perception of beauty by senses. Immanuel Kant took a step ahead and said that aesthetic is a judgement of beauty.

The history of aesthetics contains contributions by Plato, Aristotle, Hutcheson and Hume, Kant, Hegel, Nietzsche, Dewey, Heidegger, Croce and Collingwood, Sibley, Barthes and Derrida etc. All these intellectuals have seen aesthetics in their own way and each view is equally important to understand the basics of aesthetics.

---

[1] Megh, Ramesh Kuntal. Athato Saundarya Jigyasa. Vani Prakashan, 2001, p.6

Plato's idea about beauty was: "Beauty lies in the pleasure of sight and hearing... This is the privilege of beauty, that she is the loveliest, and also the most palpable to sight. But only a few can attain the vision to the Absolute Beauty."[2] Cicero believed that nothing is so beautiful in this world which cannot be made further more beautiful. His idea was that no beauty is perfect. St. Thomas Acquinas propagated that beauty is always in the right ratio because that's what our senses love. He said that beauty has three characters: completeness i.e. integrity or perfection, ratio i.e. proportion or harmony and brightness i.e. clarity. He added that beauty is what gives pleasure at sight, a vision and joy. Joseph Margolis compared 'beauty' in medieval and modern times, saying that medieval times saw the theory of beauty "pressed into service, somewhat articification, as a surrogate for especially aesthetic concerns".[3] According to Margolis, in modern aesthetics, "there is almost unanimous agreement that there is no sufficient uniformity in the range of what passes for the 'aesthetic' that would justify treating what falls under the blunderbuss as conceptually uniform in any notably instructive sense."

In the medieval times, the term 'aesthetic' was dealt with in very limited aspects of beauty, but if we see it in modern aesthetics, various thinkers had common things that they took into account. St. Augustine, Dante, Savonarola, and Albrecht Durer contributed to medieval aesthetics, while modern aesthetics had contributions from Croce, Samuel Alexander, Collingwood, Bosanquet, Emerson etc. Leonardo da Vinci, Vellori, and Mamiani propagated their views about beauty and aesthetics.

So, aesthetics is all about beauty and pleasure, and is related to the cognitive processes. In 1790, Kant described beauty as a subjective experience like tasting something. He

---

[2] Vajpayi, Dr. Rajendra. Saundarya. Madhya Pradesh Hindi Granth Academy Bhopal, 2009, p.45

[3] Margolis, Joseph. The Routledge Companion To Aesthetics. Taylor & Francis Group, 2005, pp 35-36

said that like taste, beauty gives a feel of pleasure immediately. He indicated that beauty is something that simply pleases a man and, thus, the judgement of beauty is free from any assumption or limited vision.

The aesthetics for any form of art involves inherent perceptions along with some intentional assumptions of emotion attached to prior experiences of user or producer. In my view, comprehension, comparison and decision of particular traits or characters at a certain place of any artistic creation make up aesthetics.

CHORDS

Chords are a combination of three or more notes to reach a desired harmonic sound. It is the basic unit by which the orchestration goes towards the harmonic progression, in general. The basic structure is a triad, a major, and all other chords are named or constructed on the basis of a major chord. The major chord is made up of the root note: perfect third and perfect fifth. There are many types of chords, depending on the intervallic relations of the note. Simple chords are triad i.e., major and minor. Three other triads are suspended, augmented and diminished, but these are complex chords in terms of intervallic harmonic tension. The major chord is the most relaxed intervallic structure of notes. All these aspects of chords will be discussed in the subsequent chapters.

In modern music, chords are used in shapes, like extensions, blends of two chords etc. to get newer harmonic levels, especially in jazz and blues. In the last century, more freeness in harmonic progressions has provided an open field to use chords in such a way that leads to dominate the basic principles of harmony.

Moving on the nomenclature of the chords, there are no golden rules for naming a chord. But simply, a chord can be named on the basis of the root note and all other extensions may be included. Basic nomenclature depends on the major chord, which is a basic triad. So, it is all about analysing the intervals between the notes of the chord. Each of these intervals are semitones. The acceptance of these semitone intervals is also related to the cultural aesthetic values of music in the particular region, country or landscape. So, it is better to understand the intervallic relation of notes as well as the cultural traditions if someone wants to deeply study chords. One will have to develop the skill of hearing the harmonies if he is trying to understand chords, because, after learning the basics, the interpretation of personalised definitions of intervallic colors can only be made through the developed, harmonic ears. The intervallic relations of notes of a chord are the result of consonance and dissonance, which leads to different kinds of harmony. So, the chord is a frame of a particular harmony.

Chords are classified as:

Triads i.e. major, minor, suspended, diminished and augmented.

Four note chords i.e. seventh (dominant seventh), major seventh, sixth, diminished seventh, half diminished seventh, augmented seventh, augmented major seventh, added tone chords like added ninth, added eleventh, and added thirteenth.

Five and above notes chords i.e. ninth, eleventh, thirteenth.

Altered chords i.e. chromatically-altered chords of four and above notes. Apart from that, there are poly chords i.e. combination of two chords.

Apart from the different names of chords, chords are also classified on the basis of their degree in a progression, in relation to the root note or chord. These are tonic, subdominant parallel, dominant parallel, sub dominant, and dominant parallel tonic in this reference. All these aspects of chords are broadly discussed in the next chapter, which gives a clearer idea about almost everything you need to know about chords, including the types, classification, aesthetics, impact, sound physics, chord progression, perception about moods, and use in Indian film composer's music.

AESTHETICS OF CHORDS

The combination of three or more notes is called a chord. Generally, when the thought about the beauty of chords crosses a layman's mind, he simply thinks about the chord's strumming sound or a chord progression or something similar. It always involves pleasantness of the sound of a chord. Our mind conducts psycho-analysis to decide what we love or hate. Hence, the aesthetics of chords is all about the decision-making with respect to the pleasantness of sound of basic or alternative chords for the most-lovable sound. It is a selection process, and a result of a quest for ultimate beauty. The composer strives to use alternative progression for alternative chords, including accidental notes and cadences. He also works on the ways to blend these into basic progression according to the tune. Simultaneously, the composer works on the selection of texture of sound for the chords for the whole orchestration. He works on the voicing of chords and its segmentation for different instruments. He also predicts the effectiveness of the particular chord in specific segmentation or combination of instruments.

The aesthetics of chords can be developed and groomed by having the best knowledge of their theoretical and practical aspects. Good exposure to different types of sound and timbre of instruments enhances the aesthetic sense. It further makes you want to learn more about different cultural trends of music and sound, and of course their acceptance.

A chord itself is the smallest harmonic composition. A single chord may give pleasure if it is used in a different manner in a sequence. If we play a chord, say C_m, just a single stroke of it, and then add the strumming of guitar, then further add some arpeggio patterns, the voicing of pitches and a different instrument's timbre, it will sound pleasing if planned properly.

A composer sees a chord as a part of a composition or an orchestration. The broader the knowledge and experience of the composer, the more will he be efficient in selecting a chord. When the matter is about chord progression, then the selection of accidental chords, alternative chords, extensions of chords, power chords is also very important.

From the point of view of a composer, the aesthetics of chords is simply proportional to his knowledge, experience and exposure. Richer knowledge, experience and exposure to music also means more perfection in the aesthetic sense of a composer. As discussed earlier, there is no such tool to measure the aesthetic sense, but the beauty of a creation reflects the competency of a composer, especially in terms of creativity and aesthetics.

ORCHESTRATION

Orchestration is an integral part of music and it is practiced in two ways either along with composing or after making the basic melody. Usually, orchestration comes into the making of Indian film music after the composition and lyrics are finalised. Orchestration is a musical planning for presentation of a musical thought i.e. composition. It actually is amalgamated with the process of music composition as far as its education and tradition is concerned, but in Indian film music, it comes after the creation of melody and lyrics. And, then manifestation of ideas takes place with sound design, music arrangement and recording.

The orchestrator has to be able to match the thought level of a composer so that he can justify himself in the place of the composer. Many factors can affect the quality of an orchestra. The quality of instruments, players, hall acoustics, and several mechanical and physical influences can affect the aesthetic results of an orchestration. A thorough knowledge of instruments and orchestration techniques is necessary to make a beautiful orchestration. Lessons, practice and experiences are needed to do better on the aesthetics part. A highly-skilled orchestrator should be able to work by putting himself in the place of a composer and take decisions accordingly. The golden era of Indian film music was graced by so many talented music arrangers like Sebastian D'Souza and Anthony Gonsalves, who could work efficiently with different composers at the same time.

An orchestrator has to deal with the issues like qualitative analysis of needful instruments and orchestration, the planning, problems in orchestration (could be related to instruments, players, composition etc.). The instrumentation part works with sounds, timbres, ranges and techniques of playing each instrument. Orchestration deals with major scoring issues and techniques so as to write music for various instruments effectively. By analysing the instrumentation, an orchestrator brings clarity to his writing.

Composer Samuel Adler rightly said that by mastering the technique of orchestration, one is led to "a deeper understanding of the sensitivity with which the great masters of composition have handled the symphony orchestra and how each made this remarkable instrument serve their musical ideas in the clearest and most vivid ways."[4] Deep understanding of the art can help one comprehend the practical and aesthetical aspects of orchestration.

Orchestration is a practice by which the melody or composition is enriched by adding musical elements so as to enhance its beauty and maximise the sharpness of moods

---

[4] Adler, Samuel. The Study of Orchestration. W.W. Norton and Company, New York, London, 1989, p.4

and emotions. In the Indian film industry, it is the composer who decides the structure of melodic progression, while the orchestrator works on the harmonic progressions and ornamentation of a composition. Sebastian D'souza is hailed as one of the best music arrangers of the Indian film industry because he learnt various orchestration techniques and used them to work with top music directors.

Indian Film Music

The Indian film industry has a marvellous history which began from 1897, when the first original motion picture was shot by an Indian. *The Wrestlers*—a recording of a wrestling match in Mumbai—was the first Indian film, created by Harishchandra S. Bhatvadekar aka Save Dada. In 1912, *Pundalik* was produced as the first Indian feature film, while the first Indian native film *Raja Harishchandra* was made by Dhundiraj Govind Phalke in 1913. Alam Ara is known as the first Indian talkie and was released in 1931. It met with a huge, incomparable commercial success at the time for its music and drama. The 1932-film *Indrasabha*, one of the earliest sound films in the country, made history by featuring about 70 songs. It shows that music became a boon of Indian films at that time, and now it unarguably plays a vital role in deciding the commercial viability of a film.

Since the introduction of sound in Indian cinema, music has been one of the main ingredients in the filmmaking process. The first record of film music was produced in 1934, while films of today follow a peculiar trend of holding a standalone 'music launch' event. Playback singing is another peculiarity of Indian cinematic music, where the songs are sung by someone and the actors lip-sync it during the filming of the sequence. Actually, there are barely any films made without music. This shows that filmmakers understand the role of music in films and want to keep up with the demand of their audience.

Over the years, the Indian film music industry has seen a magnificent growth in terms of quality in all aspects. If we look at the production of music, from 1931 till the present time, the industry has seen a complete change in styles, orchestration, recording, composition or any other field concerning film music. This transition was triggered by experimentation, and subsequently, a fast-changing scenario which incorporated many global styles of music into Indian cinema. The film music scene in India is still evolving, thanks to new talent and technologies.

It can be said that the Indian film music has now become a genre in itself, and the industry manages to churn out songs that the audience is able to relate to, year-after-year. The foundation was laid in the late 1940s, when our film music gained worldwide recognition, opening doors for commercial aspects to step into music production. The development of styles is still a continuous process; everyday, music composers experiment with different blends of styles and forms. Today, because of digitisation and social media, Indian cinematic music has a huge fan following across the globe. This has been discussed at length in the coming chapters.

AESTHETICS OF MUSIC

The working of aesthetics in music is a process which starts from hearing music and getting it interpreted by the mind—which conducts psycho-neuro analysis. This interpretation is then converted into an internal reaction, which comes in the form of a feeling and/or thought. To study how the aesthetics have worked, one will need to see to what extent have the thoughts of the composer and the listener matched.

For a large chunk of composers, aesthetics are a prime drive in order to get to the right audience for a certain composition. However, even for the most experienced composers, it is difficult to predict how a certain composition will be received by the listeners. One should know that the aesthetics of film music differs from other core music genres because it is totally created to support a film, and takes into account the situational demands.

In music, beauty is a relatively interpretive term. Two people's tastes in music can always be different as it is a matter of choice. The likes and dislikes in music depends on factors like the listener's knowledge and experience with different kinds of music, his psycho-analytical approach, etc.

Music is a two-way communication process between a composer and a listener, and both the ends are equally involved but both cannot control it completely. The listener, though a passive partner of tunemaking, is very important for the composer because his work will have no value without an audience. The listener has the right to accept, reject, like or dislike the composition. So, every composer has to understand his audience and should be open to receiving the demands.

What qualifies as 'good music'? The question itself is complicated and so is the answer. In any field, aesthetics do not work in isolation when deciding the 'goodness' of an object or a work of art; one's judgment is broadly based on his own life experiences. The same is applicable in the aesthetics of music. A composer needs to have empathy—the ability to understand the feelings of others—for his work to have an aesthetic value. To have aesthetics, one needs to have self actualisation—to some extent—which comes with attention, interpretation and understanding of sound and it's aura.

TUNE / MELODY

Generally, 'tune' is seen to be an overall music composition. It is like a story or a thought, complete on its own. We can say that tune is a big musical structure, which contains a combination of various multiple melodies and harmonies all together.

Melody is a linear sequence of tones, arranged in a beautiful manner aiming towards pleasant sound and mood. It is generally treated as an antonym of harmony, and can also be called as the skeletal part of tune. A tune is a combination of melody and harmony. Sometimes, a solo piece of an instrument is also called a tune. Melody and harmony are not separable when a composer works on the tunemaking.

In Indian film music, a tune or *dhun* refers to both the melody itself and the whole composition. When it is said that a music director is working on a tune for a script, or lyrics, it means that he is making a composition or a musical structure. So in the case of the industry, there is no fixed definition of tune.

The two parts of a tune or composition, i.e. melody and harmony, are discussed in Indian music theories also. Melody is referred to as 'Swar Madhurya' and harmony is treated as 'Swar Samvad'. These are Indian terms, which are also self explanatory. So, the tune is a musical story in which the melodies and harmonies, along with all other musical elements (including rhythmic inputs), act as sentences.

Tune Making

In Indian film music, making a musical composition is called 'tunemaking', or *'dhun-banana'* in Hindi. The making of a tune is always administered by a thought process, though the style may vary from person to person. Still, there are certain elements which regulate the whole process. I believe that this thought process involves the steps like perception-building, coming up with a theme, developing it to a musical structure, reaching a perfect tune, testing for acceptance, and presentation design of a tune. The acceptance of these steps, however, is subjective.

Composing a song or making a tune is an extraordinary task. Musical elements are used to add expressions and emotions to the lyrics. This has been discussed in detail in the third chapter of this book, along with some aspects of Indian film music making process like testing for acceptance and the 'mass appeal' factor. Music composer S.D. Burman used to perform his basic tune structure to his peon, driver and others close to him, to get an idea of his work's general mass appeal. Usually, the music directors end up working in either of the two situations in Indian film industry: they are either told to compose a tune for specific lyrics, or they are told to compose a tune without the lyrics, with briefing of characters, situation, mood etc.

The tune-making process for Indian films is rather difficult because the composer has to take all the briefings into account for the shoot of the song. It includes visualising the shoot and the shots for the particular song, which makes it different and more challenging in comparison to composing for a music album. The trend of playback singing for actors is also what makes the process of tunemaking in India unique.

Chapter 2

Chords

"Chords can make a different progression, different pattern altogether. When I do this, I try to do what has not been done before. Not the same formula goes every time. Second most important thing after melody is the counterpoint or what you call obbligato. Sometimes Obbligato also has to make some nice melody. Sometimes I feel, due this particular chord, I am not getting the correct obbligato. I will change the chord."

-Kersi Lord

Principles and Theories of Chord Formation

'Chord', a well-known term in the world of music, is a combination of three or more notes. In my opinion, a chord is the smallest kind of composition. Like how sentences comprise words, a harmony or a chord progression is made up of chords. The bunch of notes in a chord are arranged in a way that they fulfil the need of a musical sound.

There is no golden rule in the making of chords. However, the steps involved in creating a chord include reading, analysing and counting the intervals between the notes, and correlation between their harmonic or inharmonic sounds. These intervals can also be seen as the distance between the notes. All these distances or intervals are measured in the form of semitones. In an equally-tempered scale, an octave is made up of seven basic notes or twelve semitones.

Since we are discussing the formation of chords, we have to look at the major chord first, as it can be treated as a basic structure. A major chord is a triad made up of three notes i.e, 1st, 3rd, 5th. In the major scale, from the root note, the 3rd one is four semitones away, while 5th is seven semitones away. Normally, it is named after the name of the root note only and sometimes it is named as the particular root note + 'major' chord. For example, C chord—which comprises the notes C, E and G—is also called C major; the 'major' suffix is often not mentioned in the case of a major chord.

To make a chord, one needs to calculate and evaluate the intervals between notes to create the desired musical sound. The evaluation of intervals totally depends on one's understanding of aesthetics. Sometimes, in some musical styles, the particular intervals can be treated as non-harmonic sounds, while the same intervals are used in different styles as distinctive parts. For example, in the blues genre, the chord progressions are sometimes made up with all $7^{th}/6^{th}$ chords, but this style is not much acceptable in Indian music. Sometimes these intervals are evaluated more on the aesthetic values, than their harmonic values. This acceptance or denial is a result of the 'consonance and dissonance' effect.

Some particular intervals—like thirds, fifth, and sevenths—sound better because of a certain calculative proportionate relationship between different frequencies of notes, which sound more harmonious than other combinations of intervals like sixth, second etc. 'Pleasant' sounds depend on this relationship between intervals, and, certainly, on the cultural and ethnic factors (one's exposure to folk and country music).

Every culture passes on its own aesthetics to its art forms, including music. Some formulas have been around for long enough to make certain chords be seen and accepted as the basics of chord formations. Apart from the aesthetic values, the count of intervals is also important while forming a chord. One can create chords is an easier way if he has the knowledge about intervals. Here is a look at the conventional names for semitones:

Semitone	Interval
0	Unison
1	Flat 2nd
2	2nd
3	Minor 3rd/ augmented 2nd
4	Major 3rd
5	Perfect 4th

6	Flat 5th (Diminished 5th or augmented 4th)
7	Perfect 5th
8	Minor 6th/ augmented 5th
9	Major 6th
10	Minor 7th (Flat 7th)/ augmented 6th
11	Major 7th
12	Octave
13	Flat 9th
14	9th
15	Minor 10th (augmented 9th)
16	Major 10th
17	11th
18	Augmented 11th/diminished or flat 12th
19	Perfect 12th
20	Flat 13th/augmented 12th
21	13th

All chords are formed by using these intervals. If you want to make or play a chord, you can use the above table for reference. Understanding the intervallic sounds helps a composer develop a musical expression and perceive intervallic colours. Though formation of chords always has something to do with aesthetics, the basic idea behind that, as mentioned before, is evaluating and calculating the intervals to find a suitable sound. This evaluation and calculation is done on the basis of ratio between two intervals which has been followed for a long time.

According to studies, the Pythagorean relationship of different numbers and musical tones has been used since ancient times to create various musical compositions. Mathematicians were also known to teach music in the medieval era. It reveals the importance of mathematics for a musician.

Making compositions or playing instruments is always a mathematical practice of musical notes in form of addition, extension, repetition etc. and of course, it happens unconsciously. The great composer J. S. Bach had a strong affinity towards the practice of denoting different numbers in his compositions. In Indian classical music, too, there are many musicians who, at their best, play with number games and calculative demonstration like *aad, sawa gun* (1.25 times speed), *dedh gun* (1.5 times speed), *paun gun* (0.75 times speed), *sawa do gun* (2.25 times speed) etc. in relation to basic tempo, in the form of *laya* (tempo) or *taan* (a melodic structure of particular length) or in any of musical origination like this at the time of recitals as well as in lectures.

The basic chords are called triads (because they are made of 3 notes), and produce the basic harmonic sound. The basic chord and basic triad is the major of any key, on which other triads can be conceptualised. The other triads are minor, suspended, diminished and augmented chords.

To make a minor, the 3rd note of a major scale is flattened—which means the minor chord has the flat 3rd note. As per intervallic manner, the minor triad is made up of root, three semitones and then seven semitones. So at a glance-

Major:

Root = 0,
3rd note = 4 semitones,
5th note = 7 semitones

Minor:

Root = 0,
3rd note (minor or flat 3rd) = 3 semitones,
5th notes = 7 semitones

Suspended triads: suspend 3rd note of major triads, replacing it by either 2nd note or 4th note of the same major scale. Apart from the giving colour to a major or a minor chord, suspension of a note also gives a different kind of sound. A suspended chord has a unique way of blending two harmonies. See this blend in the following example:

C sus4: In this chord, the 3rd note is suspended and replaced by the 4th note i.e., F, so the notes of C sus4 are C F G.

Now, let's see the harmonic balance of the chord. The C makes harmony with its 5th i.e. G, and the F also makes harmony with its 5th i.e. C. So, it means C sus4 has two notes which act like perfect 5th to create a harmony.

Also, we can look at C sus2, where the notes that are used are: C D G. Here, C has its perfect 5th i.e. G, and G also has its perfect 5th i.e. D. These are the intervallic values of the suspended chords:

For Suspended 4th

Root = 0, 4th note = 5 semitones, 5th note = 7 semitones

For Suspended 2nd

Root = 0, 2nd note = 2 semitones, 5th note = 7 semitones

The next triad we'll discuss is 'diminished'. Diminution means minimising the intervals. To make a diminished chord, the 3rd and 5th are flattened. So, the intervals of a diminished are:

Root = 0, 3rd note (flat 3rd) = 3 semitones, 5th note (flat 5th) = 6 semitones

In C dim, the notes are:

C	E♭ (flat E or flat 3rd)	G♭ (flat G or flat 5th)
Root = 0	= 3 semitones	= 6 semitones

When the 7th chord is made as diminished, then it is called diminished 7th. These are its intervallic values:

Root   3rd note (flat 3rd)   5th note (flat 5th)   7th note (flat flat 7th)
= 0   = 3 semitones   = 6 semitones   = 9 semitones

So, if we consider C diminished 7th, then it will have these notes:

C	E♭	G♭	A
Root	3	6	9

The reason behind using the double flat 7th is very clear. In the basic 7th chord of a triad, the flat 7th note is already used, and it is flattened by an extra semitone for diminution. It can be called a perfect 6th as well, but because we are minimising every note, it is considered as double flat 7th.

An interesting fact about the diminished 7th is that its intervallic pattern is 0-3-6-9. If the root is omitted, then the 3rd semitone becomes a root for the next 3 notes and it has the same intervallic pattern i.e. 0-3-6 semitones means a diminished chord. When it's 7th is made, then it also has the same intervallic pattern i.e., 0-3-6-9. Let's look at an example for a clearer view:

C	E♭	G♭	A
Root	3	6	9

When C is omitted, then we get:

E♭	G♭	A
0	3	6

Now 7th of this E♭ diminished is:

E♭	G♭	A	C
0	3	6	9

So, the thing is that both Cdim7 and E♭dim7 use similar notes. It further happen with each note i.e. G♭ and A, when made it diminished 7th.

The last type of triads to be discussed are augmented chords. In augmentation, the note is made sharp. The last note of this triad is a sharp 5th. The intervallic value for augmented triad is:

Root=0,   3rd note = 4 semitones,
5th note (sharp 5th) = 8 semitones

If we see the C aug, then it will have the notes –

C	E	G♯ 5th note
(Root)	(perfect 3rd note)	(sharp 5th)
0	4 semitones	8 semitones

Here ends the discussion on triads. Now we'll move to another category: seventh chords. Though we already talk about the seventh chord while learning about diminished and augmented chords, this section will further elaborate on the seventh chords.

As the name suggests, a seventh chord includes a 7th note, which is added to a triad. Sevenths are of two types i.e. 7th or dominant 7th, and major 7th. When the flat 7th note of a major scale is added to a triad, it becomes 7th chord or dominant 7th chord. When the perfect 7th note of a major scale is added with a triad, it is called a major 7th chord. Now, why is it called a dominant 7th when it uses a flat 7th note? This is because on a major scale's dominant note (e.g. G on C scale), the modal movement (mixolydian mode) goes to 7th note F, which actually is a flat 7th of G major scale (and not a perfect 7th i.e., F♯). So, actually, it is dominant's 7th and not 'dominant 7th'. This idea is used on major as well as other scales too for aesthetic reasons. These 7th chords can be created on a major chord and, as well as, a minor chord.

The intervallic values for these 7th chords are as follows:

Major triad + flat 7th = 7th chord =

root	3rd	5th	7th (flat)
0	4	7	10

e.g,–
C major + flat 7th = C7th =

C	E	G	B♭

Major triads + perfect 7th = major 7th =

root	3rd	5th	7th (perfect)
0	4	7	11

e.g.– C major + perfect 7th = C major 7th =

C	E	G	B

Since we have discussed the 7th chord of diminished, here is a small illustration of the intervallic pattern for augmented 7th. Basically, the 7th chord of any triad contains a flat 7th note. So, the augmented 7th chord has intervallic values as mentioned here:

Root	3rd (perfect 3rd)	5th (sharp 5th)	7th (flat 7th)
= 0	= 4	= 8	= 10

If we make the 7th of C aug, then the notes comes in this system:

C	E	G♯	B
Root	(perfect 3rd)	(sharp 5th)	(flat 7th)
= 0	= 4	= 8	= 10

Let's see minor triads from the aspect of 7th chords:

Minor triads + flat 7th = Minor 7th =

Root	3rd (flat 3rd)	5th	7th (flat)
0	3	7	10

e.g.,

C minor + flat 7th = C Minor 7th =

C	E♭	G	B♭

Minor triads + perfect 7th = Minor Major 7th =

Root	3rd (flat 3rd)	5th	7th (perfect)
0	3	7	11

e.g.,

C minor + perfect 7th = C minor major 7th

C	E♭	G	B

In the seventh chords, there is an augmented major 7th also, where augmented chord is exposed along with the perfect 7th note. It is also called the major seventh sharp fifth chord.

There are many chords to look at when we discuss intervallic calculations like 9th, 11th, 13th chords, 6th chords, 6/9 chords, major 9th, 11th, 13th chords, added chords, altered chords etc. 9th, 11th, and 13th chords are basically made on the 7th (or dominant 7th chords), either on major or minor triads 7th chords on which the perfect 9th (2nd on the next octave), perfect 11th (4th on the next octave) and perfect 13th (6th on the next octave) notes are introduced. The basic intervallic values are the same as we discussed in 7th chords, along with the intervals of 9th (14th semitones), 11th (17th semitones), and 13th (21st semitones).

For example, if we look at C9, C11, C13 chords:

C9:

C7 (C dominant 7th) + 9th =

C	E	G	B♭	D
0	4	7	10	14

C11:

C9 + 11th =

C	E	G	B♭	D	F (1 octave above)
0	4	7	10	14	17 (1 octave above)

C13:

C11 + 13th =

C	E	G	B♭	D	F	A (1 octave above)
0	4	7	10	14	17	21 (1 octave above)

The point to be noted is that there is a difference between 9th, 11th, and 13th chords, and major 9th, 11th, and 13th chords. The major 9th, 11th, and 13th chords are made on the basic chord, major 7th, which contains the perfect 7th. So, if we have to find major 9th, 11th, 13th, then we have to calculate the intervals as follows:

Major 9th

Root	3rd note	5th note	perfect 7th note	9th note
0	4	7	11	14

Major 11th

Root	3rd note	5th note	perfect 7th note	9th note	11th note
0	4	7	11	14	17

Major 13th

Root	3rd note	5th note	perfect 7th note	9th note	11th note	13th note
0	4	7	11	14	17	21

So, the above figures show how the 9th, 11th, and 13th chords can be made. Now, let's discuss the intervallic calculation of the 6th chord. As the name suggests, it includes a perfect 6th note of a major scale. A perfect 6th is made up of ninth semitone. For a 6th chord, whether it is a major triad or a minor triad, the perfect 6th note will always be used.

For a major 6th:

Root	3rd note	5th note	6th note
0	4	7	9

On the key of C, the C6 will be C, E, G, A.

For a minor 6th:

Root	flat 3rd note	5th note	6th note
0	3	7	9

For the key of C, the C minor 6th will be:

C, E♭ G, A

Coming to the 6/9 chords, they have a basic 6th chord with an added 9th note. So, their intervallic values will be:

For a major triad:

Root	3rd note	5th note	6th note	9th note
0	4	7	9	14

If we choose the C key, then it will be:

C	E	G	A	D
0	4	7	9	14

For a minor triad, the 6/9 chord will be:

Root	minor 3rd note	5th note	6th note	9th note
0	3	7	9	14

So, for a C_m 6/9, these notes will be used:

C	E♭	G	A	D
0	3	7	9	14

Now, let's move on to 'added chords'. Added chords, simply, just have an added note. For example, if we look at 'C add 2', it has the 2nd note added to a C major chord. So, its intervallic values will be as follows, on the basis of which every added chord can be calculated:

C add 2 =	C major + 2nd			
=	Root	3rd note	5th note	+2nd note
Or	Root	2nd	3rd	5th
	0	2	4	7

Similarly, for C minor add 2, it will be:

C minor add 2 =	C minor + 2nd			
	Root	2nd	3rd	5th
	0	2	3	7

Many times, people get confused between 'C add2' and 'C add9'. This is because they both have the same note (2 and 9 being basically the same), but in different octaves. Therefore, it is better to calculate them on the basis of their intervals to avoid confusion.

Sometimes, C add2 is also misunderstood as a suspended chord, but one should know that the 3rd is omitted in a suspended chord, while an added chord contains it.

Another popular chords that are confused with each other 'C9' and 'C add 9'. To be clear about them, always keep in mind that 'C9' has a basic chord—'C7'—in addition to the 9th note, which contains a flat 7th; 'C add 9', on the other hand, only includes C major notes with the 9th note.

For a clearer picture, here's an example:

C9	=	C7 + 9th	= C E G B♭ D
C add 9	=	C + 9th	= C E G D

What is essential is that one should always keep intervallic values of a chord in mind to make the right chord while writing. If you are using a unique combination, always name it right by calculating the intervals used.

We will now discuss altered chords, which are a result of a chromatic alteration of the notes in any predefined chord. If we want to turn 'C9' into 'C9♯ or 'C9♭, then this will be the scenario:

C9 = C E G B♭ D

To make C9♯, the 9th note, i.e. D, is made sharper by one semitone:

C9♯ = C E G B♭ D♯

To make C9♭, use a flat 9th:

C9♭ = C E G B♭ D♭

There are no restrictions in making altered chords as their use depends on the aesthetic needs and one's thirst to obtain new sound and harmonic structure.

Here, we end the basic theoretical discussion about the formation of a particular chord. These formations are usually done on the basis of calculations of intervals between the different notes used to form a combination to fulfil a need of musical sound. Depending totally on the aesthetics, the chords can also be formed to fulfil the need of a particular motif.

Sound Physics of Notes & Chords

Two tones produced with a smaller frequency ratio create better consonance i.e., smaller number of ratio of frequencies gives better consonance of sound and so the saturated harmonies or stable sonority comes out. Sir James Jeans discussed as below[5] describing the frequency ratio of notes, under the discussion of concord associated with small numbers;

Interval	Frequency Ratio	Largest Number Occurring in ratio
Unison	1:1	1
Octave	2:1	2
Fifth	3:2	3
Fourth	4:3	4
Major Third	5:4	5
Major Sixth	5:3	5
Minor Third	6:5	6
Minor Sixth	8:5	8
Second	9:8	9

The ratio has been discussed in light of the Pythagorean doctrine. Sir James Jeans discussed many theories about harmony of chord. One of these theories was Euler's theory of Harmony. This theory argued that coherence or law and order in the feeling of a particular trait or aspect is a natural phenomenon of the human brain. On the basis of this argument, consonance and dissonance of sound and harmonies was propagated. But, this theory has drawn many criticisms.

---

[5] Jeans, Sir James. Science and Music. Cambridge University Press, 1961, p.154

French mathematician Jean le Rond d'Alembert theorised that the fundamental tone has its natural second harmonic i.e., octave, and third harmonic i.e., twelfth. He said that the octave and twelfth i.e., fifth were the most consonant naturally.

German physicist Hermann von Helmholtz has also defined the harmony of chords as consonance and dissonance in terms of beats. The first harmonic relation between notes was discussed by Pythagoras, whose observations of vibrating strings helped mankind understand acoustics.

The division of a string in nodes at halfway, one third, one fourth and so on, produces a particular tone called overtones. With the first node, the produced tone is one octave higher. When the string is divided into 3 equal parts by two nodes, the produced overtone is the fifth note of the scale but in the next higher octave. Further, 4 equal part divisions by 3 nodes gives us the second octave note. To divide the string in 5 equal parts by 4 nodes, it gives us the third note in the third higher octave. Now, if we bring all these notes into a series by overlooking the octave leap, then we get the basic fundamental triad notes i.e., first, third and fifth creates a major chord. I think that's why the major chord is the most relaxed and stable structure in harmonies because it consists of three basic overtones.

All chords are produced because of certain vibrations in the constituent notes. This result, which may either be consonance or dissonance, gives an idea about the stability or tension of the chord structure and the progression of chords.

Basically, when something vibrates, a sound is produced and the object passes its vibration to the medium like water, air etc. This vibration travels in the medium and forms a wave, which can be heard. Sound waves have two basic features which are called compression and rarefaction. The high pressure or density area is compression and low pressure and density area is rarefaction.

The unit of measurement for a sound wave is called a wavelength. The wavelength is a measurement between two peak points of the wave, or in an easier way, we can say that it is a distance between two compressions or two rarefactions. The wavelength and speed of the wave determines pitch or frequency of the sound. Wavelength, frequency and the speed are related in the following way:

Speed = Frequency x Wavelength

Hence, the longer the wavelength, the lower the pitch. The loudness of a sound is determined by its amplitude i.e. the height of the wave. Generally, the things which can produce vibrations have at least one state in which they may remain at rest. This state is called equilibrium. When disturbed while at equilibrium, the object is dragged back to rest by the restoring force. In the meantime, to come back to rest, the object moves at a certain speed, overshooting the rest position and moves on to the other side. This motion is called oscillation. When the amplitude of the oscillator is very small (in nanometres), the to and fro motion is called vibration. Sir James Jeans called a vibration "a special kind of oscillation", but added that vibrations possess "certain very simple properties which are not possessed by oscillations in general."[6]

In oscillation, the distance covered by the object from the position of rest is dominated by the restoring force which will pull it back, while in vibration, the restoring force is proportional to distance from the position of rest. In this relation, the motion developed is called simple harmonic motion or SHM.

Another term in sound physics that musicians should know is resonance. In Latin, resonances means 'resound' i.e. to sound out together. An object vibrating at the same natural frequency of a second object forces that second object to go

---

[6] Jeans, Sir James. Science and Music. Cambridge University Press, 1961, p.29

into the motion with vibration. This is resonance. When a forced vibration is produced, resonance takes place. Musical instruments also produce sound due to resonance.

TYPES OF CHORDS AND ITS CLASSIFICATION

The chord is a combination of different pitches where three or more notes are played simultaneously as a block. Chords are made up on the basis of interval between these notes which are administered by consonance and dissonance. Consonance and dissonance are the basics of harmony. That's why chords can be called as the frames of harmony.

The types of chord are:

1. TRIADS
   a. Major
   b. Minor
   c. Suspended
   d. Diminished
   e. Augmented
2. FOUR NOTE CHORDS
   a. Seventh (dominant seventh)
   b. Major seventh
   c. Sixth
   d. Diminished seventh
   e. Half diminished seventh
   f. Augmented seventh
   g. Added tones chords like added $9^{th}/11^{th}/13^{th}$
3. CHORDS WITH FIVE OR MORE NOTES:
   a. Ninth
   b. Eleventh
   c. Thirteenth
4. ALTERED CHORDS: The chords with four or more notes that have chromatically-altered notes as flat or sharp.

TRIADS: A chord of three notes is called a triad. Such chords may be major, minor, suspended, diminished and augmented by the nature of the harmonic sounds. The intervals of these chords have been discussed earlier in this book.

FOUR NOTE CHORDS: These are chords which have four notes, like the seventh which has flat 7th with either a major or a minor triad. The major seventh has the perfect 7th note. The sixth chord includes the perfect sixth with a major or minor triad. Diminished 7th, augmented 7th, augmented major 7th and added tone chords with 9th, 11th or 13th are the other chords which have four notes.

CHORDS WITH FIVE OR MORE NOTES: These are the chords which came into use by experimentation of pitch classes in the triads and four note chords. They can together be called complex chords. Under the example of such chords are the 9th, 11th and 13th chords. These are extended chords. Reaching on the 13th extension, the experimentation gets tougher as at this point all the seven notes of a key get involved in the scale and the further inclusion of notes seems impossible. Normally, the first four notes of these chords come from the first octave of the key, while the next notes are introduced in the next octave of the key.

ALTERED CHORDS: In these chords, 5th, 9th, 11th and 13th notes can be altered chromatically by flattening and sharpening these notes. These chords are used in jazz and blues.

ADDED TONE CHORDS: These chords are made up of triads and an added tone like second, fourth, sixth, ninth, eleventh, etc. These are written with the suffix 'add', like 'C add9'. Chords like added 9th, added 11th and added 13th may be confused with 9th, 11th and 13th. When we say C ninth (C9), it is a chord made up of the C seventh with addition of 9th. So, it contains the notes C E G B♭ D, while 'C add9' is just C major with addition of 9th i.e., C E G and D in the upper octave.

POLYCHORDS: A polychord is a combination of two chords, one on top of another. These are bitonal or polytonal in nature. If E♭m is placed over Fm, then it would be written as E♭m/Fm. Basically, these chords are extended chords.

MYSTIC CHORDS: The mystic chord is also known as Prometheus chord. It contains six notes and sounds very dissonant. The structure of this chord is C F♯ B♭ E A D. So, it can be interpreted as a quartalhexa chord as it comprises an augmented fourth, diminished fourth, augmented fourth, perfect fourth and another perfect fourth. Russian composer Alexander Scriabin used mystic chords in his compositions. From the C key, it is constructed with the notes C, F♯, B♭, E, A and D.

PETRUSHKA CHORD: Russian composer Igor Stravinsky used this structure in his ballet 'Petrushka' and other tunes. It consists of a C major chord with an F♯ major, and it sounds very dissonant. The notes used are: C E G / F♯ A♯ C♯.

PSALMS CHORD: This chord was used by Stravinsky in his composition, Symphony of Psalms. It involves root along with minor third, perfect fifth and minor tenth. Minor tenth is just a minor third placed octave higher. It was an opening chord in that composition. It is also called barking E minor.

TRISTAN CHORD: This chord is like a half-diminished seventh chord. It includes the root note with the intervals of augmented fourth, augmented sixth and augmented second. The chord is made of the notes: F B D♯ and G♯. Richard Wagner used this structure in his composition *Tristan and Isolde*.

HENDRIX CHORD: The dominant seventh sharp ninth chord is named as Hendrix chord due to its excessive use by rock guitarist Jimi Hendrix. It produces harmonic tension of major third and sharp ninth i.e. minor third in higher octave.

These are the main chords which are usually brought into the discussion on the types of chords.

CLASSIFICATION OF CHORDS

The classification of chords is a matter of a functional harmonic system of different virtual pitches in a given key. The roman numeral system is mostly used for the classification of chords based on the numbering of chords in a major key. Hofmann-Engl created a model for a virtual pitch on a given key.[7] They examined a chord with its overtone series and made the best matches according to frequencies. The key of C, for example, has six main chords i.e., C major, D minor, E minor, F major, G major and A minor chords. In the Roman numeral, these are numbered as follows:

C major – I
D minor – II
E minor – III
F major – IV
G major – V
A minor – VI

This classification does not show any harmonic relation between the chords. Riemann (1880) proposed this classification on the basis of functional harmony. All these chords were named on the basis of the constructional functional relation between them. These are the names of chords given by him:

C major – I – Tonic
D minor – II – Sub-dominant Parallel
E minor – III – Dominant Parallel
F major – IV – Sub-dominant
G major – V – Dominant
A minor – VI – Parallel Tonic

---

[7] Hofmann-Engl, Ludger. Virtual Pitch and the Classification of Chords in Minor and Major Keys. http://www.chameleongroup.org.uk/research/ICMPC_10.pdf

The Riemann system recognised the tension between chord I (tonic) and chord V (dominant) as a central feature of tonal music.

Riemann also saw different cadences as a tension-and-release process between different degrees of chords. It is more oriented towards aesthetic satisfaction and a musical ear can understand this classification.

Nowadays, the chords are classified as under (in comparison of Roman system and Riemann system):

With the key C for major scale:

Key	Roman N. Sys	Riemann System	Current Terminology
C	I	Tonic	Tonic
D	II	Sub-dominant Parallel	Sub-mediant/ Supertonic
E	III	Dominant Parallel	Mediant
F	IV	Sub-dominant	Sub-dominant
G	V	Dominant	Dominant
A	VI	Parallel Tonic	Super-dominant
B	VII	-	Leading tone

Trending Minor Scales

In the minor scale, there are three usually trending scales: natural, harmonic, and melodic minor. In the key C, natural minor has 3 flat notes (like C D E♭ F G A♭ B♭) in comparison to major scale. In harmonic minor, the seventh note gets sharp by one semitone (i.e., B♭ to B both in ascending and descending order.

In melodic minor scale, sixth and seventh notes get sharp by one semitone each in ascending, while in descending, it is just like natural minor (like C D E♭ F G A B/ C B♭ A♭ G F E♭ D C).

In different scales, notes become flat or sharp and the chord gets variation (in terms of major, minor, diminished, augmented, 7th, etc.) but the naming based on degrees remains as their serial number of notes. Their degrees are tonic, submediant, mediant, subdominant, dominant, super dominant, and leading notes.

More About Chord Progression

(Scales, Degrees & Modes)

The chord sequence is a planned variety of chords in a given key or scale. Normally, we know these sequences as chord progressions. A chord progression is an arrangement of chords like words in sentences. It has a certain musical aim to accomplish, without which no progression can be worthy of existing.

Chord progression can work in two ways, either it can establish a tonality or contradict it. Arnold Schoenberg argued that the combination of harmonies which make a progression depend on the function which has to be performed (could be establishment, modulation, transition, contrast or reaffirmation).[8]

A chord progression provides a basic melodic nature to the composition along with harmonic aggressions. It works as a spinal cord of harmony. It is the peculiarity of progression which represents the result of inner arguments of the composer regarding dissonance, consonance, tension and release patterns, modality, tonality, atonality etc. The effectiveness of chord progression is a result of harmonic perception. At present time, chord progressions are relatively free from any kind of limitation of root motion. Over the years, harmonic

---

[8] Schoenberg, Arnold. Structural Functions of Harmony. Faber & Faber, p.1. www.pdfdrive.com/arnold-schoenberg-structural-functions-of-harmonypdf-e33412696.html.

movements got more flexibility due to relaxed sonority construction patterns in terms of intervallic tension and its resolutions. This relaxation came into force due to a result of earlier experiments like the twelve tone system of Schoenberg which encouraged composers to take liberty in terms of sonority and harmony. This relaxation gave a freedom and musical dareness to make the root motion according to the composer's wish and to overlook the traditional patterns.

Chord progressions are basically an adaptation of harmonies in a desired manner so that usage of different types of chords can achieve a particular sonority for a definite mood or thought of a composer. It always strives to achieve musical satisfaction. Chord progressions may be made by using different chords of existing scales, modes or simply experimenting with sounds and harmonies.

In tonal music, chord progressions like I – IV – V – I are very common. It means it is a progression of a major chord. In this progression, the tonic chord is followed by the sub-dominant chord and then a dominant chord. Both the chords are major.

In a chord progression, different chords play different roles. Some chords tend to give stability, while others give departure from stability, provide harmonic tension or base to go for stability and relaxation again. Each chord progression follows the cycle of stability, tension and its resolution again towards stability. It also includes the aesthetic thirst for suitable and pleasant sonor objectives. Some common chord progressions are:

Major –

I – IV – V
I7 – ii7 – V
I7 – vi7 – ii7 – V7

Minor –

i – iv7 – v
i – ii (dim) – v
i – vi (dim) – ii – v7

(Upper case represents major chords; lower case represents minor chords.)

This representation is of a generic form of chords in a diatonic scale. Different chord progressions are created by substitution, addition, or alteration of chords in a particular progression according to the needs and aesthetics of a composer.

Example:

Major –

		Sub-dominant	Dominant	
iii	vi	[ii/IV]	[V/vii]	I

Minor –

			[ii°/iV]	[V/Vii]	
VII	III	VI	[ii°/iV]	[V/Vii]	i

SCALES

Scales can generally be conceived as a series of notes in an octave. Nowadays, the most common scale is the diatonic scale of seven notes. It is further segregated as major and minor scales. In this scale there is a range of total twelve tones in each octave.

If we start from key C, the diatonic scale goes like:

C, D, E, F, G, A, B, C

This is a major scale of C, which is the most common.

The second-most common scale is a natural minor scale which is derived from diatonic major scale. If we start from the key C, the natural minor scale is:

C, D, E♭, F, G, A♭, B♭, C

In this natural minor scale, three flat notes are in comparison to a major scale. The important fact that has to be understood is that the intervals between notes of scales are fixed regardless of the key chosen to play. The diatonic scale contains the intervals of whole, whole, half, whole, whole, whole, and half tones in order to complete an octave.

There may be a number of scales depending on the choices based on ethnicity, learning and cultural trends existing in the certain geographical musical circles. By the use of different kinds of intervallic spacings and chromatic alterations, many scales have been developed in different parts of the globe, which we recognise as Western, Irish, Indian, Eastern scales.

In diatonic scale, all the notes are named on the basis of their tonal relation with root note, also called 'degrees', as follows:

Root note	Tonic
2nd note	Supertonic
3rd note	Mediant
4th note	Sub – dominant
5th note	Dominant
6th note	Super dominant
7th note	Leading note

The series of twelve tones is called a chromatic scale. However, this is the modern scale of music. Initially, the musical scale was all about choosing the relations between different intervals of frequencies. This relation was analysed by Pythagoras. He named the intervals as unison, octave, perfect fifth and fourth. He saw some definite mathematical connections between tones to establish these intervals. And, now we know that these relations are based on frequency. The relationship established by Pythagorus, further led a strong base to form different theories regarding music.

After getting different tonal combinations depending on the intervallic relationship between notes, the various families of pitches have been used as scales like major, minor, chromatic, etc.

Modes

A mode is basically a technique which derives a new scale from another scale. The mode gets the same notes as the original scale from where it is being derived. In simple words, if we shift the tonic degree to another note of the original scale and make a movement in a fresh degree base, then it is called a mode.

There are seven modes which have been derived in theories. These are:

1. Ionian (First mode)
2. Dorian (Second mode)
3. Phrygian (Third mode)
4. Lydian (Fourth mode)
5. Mixolydian (Fifth mode)
6. Aeolian (Sifth mode)
7. Locrian (Seventh mode)

1. Ionian mode:

It is similar to Bilawal Thaat in Indian music. From the key of C, the basic major scale is called the Ionian mode. These are its notes: G, A, B, C, D, E, F.

2. DORIAN MODE:

If on the same scale, we move from D and cover the whole octave with D tonic, then it will be: D, E, F, G, A, B, C, D, which is the dorian mode. It gives a different intervallic combination from the original C tonic, despite using the same notes. Kafi Thaat is similar to it in Indian music.

The Ionian mode follows this combination of intervals:

W W H W W W H

(W = Whole tone, H = Half tone or semitone)

Meanwhile, dorian mode follows this intervallic combination:

W H W W W H W

The intervallic interpretation of dorian mode is: D- root, E- perfect 2nd, F- flat 3rd, G- perfect 4th, A- perfect 5th, B- perfect 6th and C- flat 7th. So, it gives a different musical feel from the Ionian mode.

3. PHRYGIAN MODE:

From the C scale, if we start movement from E, then the notes will be:

E, F, G, A, B, C, D and E.

The combination of intervals will be: H W W W H W W. In Indian music, Bhairavi Thaat bears resemblance to it.

The intervallic values in Phrygian mode are; E- root, F- flat 2nd, G- flat 3rd, A- perfect 4th, B- perfect 5th, C- flat 6th and D- flat 7th.

4. LYDIAN MODE:

From the same scale, C, if we move from F, then the notes will be:

F, G, A, B, C, D, E and F.

The intervals will then be: W W W H W W H. In Indian music, Yaman Thaat is similar to it. The intervallic values of lydian mode are; F- root, G- perfect 2nd, A- perfect 3rd, B- augmented 4th, C- perfect 5th, D- perfect 6th and E- perfect 7th.

5. MIXOLYDIAN MODE:

From the C scale, if the movement starts from G, then the notes will be G, A, B, C, D, E, F and G and the intervals will be, W W H W W H W. It is similar to Khamaj Thaat in Indian music.

The intervallic interpretation for mixolydian mode is: G- root, A- perfect 2nd, B- perfect 3rd, C- perfect 4th, D- perfect 5th, E- perfect 6th and F- flat 7th.

6. AEOLIAN MODE:

From the C scale, if the movement starts from A, then the notes will be:

A, B, C, D, E, F, G and A.

The intervals will be, W H W W H W W. In Indian music, Asawari Thaat is similar to this mode. The intervallic values of the aeolian mode are; A- root, B- perfect 2nd, C- flat 3rd, D- perfect 4th, E- perfect 5th, F- flat 6th and G- flat 7th.

7. LOCRIAN MODE:

From the C scale, this movement starts from B and notes comes as: B, C, D, E, F, G, A and B.

The intervals H W W H W W W are used in this mode. The intervallic values of locrian are: B-root, C- flat 2nd, D- flat 3rd, E- perfect 4th, F- flat 5th, G- flat 6th and A- flat 7th.

This is the only mode where the perfect 5th is absent. In Indian music, it may resemble the Bhairavi thaat by replacing *pancham* (perfect 5th) with *teevra madhyam* (augmented 4th). So, it can be said that this movement involves both 4th's without 5th.

AESTHETICS OF CHORDS

(Perceptions, Hypothesis, Theories and Views about Moods)

One's knowledge of chords is associated with his training in this segment of music. After learning about the broad spectrum of chords, this knowledge connects with the thought process when one has to work on a composition. The aesthetics associated with chords don't just depend on a composer's natural instinct but also training. A composer cannot achieve the aesthetic sense of chords until he gets proper training and exposure.

Harmony plays a vital role in making the composition come as a whole. Hence, it is very important to give proper attention to harmony while composing musical structures. It is important for a composer to make melody with complete awareness of chords and harmonies, so that the musical structure gets the best melodic and harmonic lines.

The aesthetics of chords is basically linked to the composer finding and choosing the best suitable chord for a particular composition or its part. A composer's aesthetics is usually developed because of training as well as the experience gained from hearing and composing music. The kind of training, hearing, and sharing of experience with other musicians helps a composer develop his aesthetics with respect to chords and music.

If writing a composition is the process of forming a sentence, then the word's knowledge and suitability is enough to reach the perfect chord for a phrase or tune. When we speak, our brain chooses the right words to express a particular thought; choosing the right chord is just similar to that. Understanding this is very simple if we have a strong vocabulary of words. The same process is adapted by our brain when it comes to judge the suitability of chords. It is all a matter of choice. The choice of chord is made with the help of knowledge and experience. Knowledge guides to a technically-sound choice and experience helps with assessing the result.

A composer's perception towards chords is totally his own discretion. However, while working on a tune, a composer may hypothecate many variants of chords, including extension, alteration, substitute, accidentals, and inversions. Along with this, the composer may also hypothecate voicings of chords, which is also a part of harmonisation and re-harmonisation of compositions. This whole discussion is basically linked with the expression of moods.

Aesthetics of Chords

Requires:

- Good exposure to different sounds and timbres of instruments.
- Good exposure to different cultures of music and sound along with their acceptance/rejection.
- Openness to accept non-musical sounds to understand contrast of good/bad sound textures.
- Acceptance of different harmonic and enharmonic sounds to feel tension of sounds and find their possible resolution to reach on relaxed harmonic structure.

```
Decide on the pleasantness of sound of alternative chords to get the most lovable sound.
          ↓
Alternative progression for the alternative chord including accidental notes and cadences. They are blended into a basic progression according to tune.
          ↓
Selection of texture of chords for the whole orchestra, like voicing and segmentation in different instruments; predicting highest effectiveness of chord in the segments of instruments.
          ↓
Judge and decide on the balance of all previous selections.
          ↓
Beauty
```

Music is broadly treated as a means of pleasure. In general, pleasure is a relative term. One piece of music may give pleasure to someone, while the same music may not give pleasure to another. Gordon Graham said, "Every piece of music of any sophistication is a construction out of certain variables – melody, harmony, rhythm and form, together with the timbre and texture of sound created by the different sounds of instruments and voices."[9] A good composer uses these variables in a manner that attracts both mass and class.

The success of a composer or his composition is based on his skill of managing all musical variants in a way which results in a perfect combination. Also, the assessment of the listener's choice and pleasure plays a major role in the success story. That is why, a great musician may or may not be a great composer.

The aesthetics related to chords and music do not give a straight-forward conclusion towards a particular mood or emotion. Rather, it enhances the imaginations of that mood in a listener through the expertise of the composer. Graham discussed the reflection of emotion by music in his 2005 book and concluded by calling expressiveness "the communication of a mental state". "Expressiveness is an imaginative way of articulating something. What is important about expressiveness in art is that it enhances our awareness," he wrote.[10]

The expressiveness of an idea depends on the things which have been imagined in a specific mood or situation. One's experience may not exactly match with his imagination, but it is certainly something that has some effect on his imagination. Expression, thus, is a propagation of things that have been imagined or need to be imagined further. So, it seeks support from the receiver's interpretive skills, too.

---

[9] Graham, Gordon. Philosophy of The Arts, An Introduction to Aesthetics. Routledge, Taylor and Francis Group, 2005, p.78.
[10] Ibid. p.83.

As any art form is highly associated with expression and imagination, that form particularly creates a bond or bridge between performer and audience (receiver) and that bond leads the receiver to imagine the particular emotion or mood. That is the important factor which decides the success or failure of any presentation or composition. In that way, the composer puts his idea in front of the receivers, who may interpret the things—through a mutually created bond between both—in different ways. Though this bond or bridge is a relative term and every listener may have a different interpretation of thoughts, in most cases, the bridge does get established. These conventional associations help groom and nourish one's aesthetic sense. All these conventional associations are essential for richer experiences, a stronger perception and more consolidated thoughts. There is no doubt that these associations affect reception of mood and emotion from music, but it is difficult to have an imagination without relevant prior experience. So, these associations are necessary to understand that mood and also to judge the constituents of construction of the bridge which links the composer's aesthetics and listener's preparation to reach till the completion of implantation of thought.

Arnold Schoenberg's view about mood is rather similar to my mindset. He said, "From the viewpoint of psychology, our capacity for mental and emotional associations is as unlimited as our capacity for repudiating them is limited. Thus, every ordinary object can provoke musical associations, and, conversely, music can evoke associations with extra musical objects."[11]

With the help of chords, the form of harmony contributes as the contrast of thoughts or emotions. Chords are a result of a quest for harmony. The progression made for the chords

---

[11] Schoenberg, Arnold. Fundamentals of Music Composition. Edited By Gerald Strang and Leonard Stein, Faber and Faber, London, Boston, 1967, p.93

and its distribution for orchestration helps enhance the mood and emotion. Many forms of music are associated with certain characters, stories, and locations etc. These forms produce not only musical impression but also an association with a definite object. Schoenberg believed that the term 'character' in music refers to the emotion which the piece should produce, the mood in which it was composed, and the manner in which it must be played.

Most of the time, the composition (i.e. planning of notes, chords and harmonies) is later enriched by its orchestration, playing, and presentation techniques. All parts are equally important for expressiveness of the mood or emotion. To the best of my knowledge, the aesthetics of chords is almost an undiscussed part of music. Chords have definitely been discussed universally at the level of their construction, naming, progression and harmonics, but not in aesthetic senses.

From my discussions with performers, I have understood that the major chord is the best 'relaxed' type of chord while the second-best relaxed chord is the minor chord. The major chord seems to have the best relaxed and energetic combination of notes as far as its sound is concerned. Though the minor chord is also very much relaxed, it reflects a little lower level energetic combination of notes. The major chord reflects full energy so it denotes happiness, while the minor chord is a little bit tensed in comparison to the major chord due to the minor third note.

I think, no chord—when played in isolation—is expressive in terms of mood or emotion. When it is played in a composition, the chord shows its effect in terms of mood, expression and beauty. Furthermore, the selection of instrument for a particular chord at a particular place of a composition is also a distinctive factor. In a composition, a single chord may give the best effect on a particular instrument. The playing technique of that particular chord may also change or enhance the effect in terms of beauty and emotion. Apart from relaxed chords i.e., major and minor, all other chords have 'tension' in terms of harmony, and sometimes these may sound unpleasant to people when played in isolation.

If a musician plays a diminished or augmented chord in isolation on any instrument, it sounds dissonant. But when a progression of a minor chord (like C minor) is played, for instance i – VII – VI – ii° – V, then, apart from ii° (D Diminished), all are relaxed chords, but the D diminished gives utmost beauty to the progression. Being a tensed chord in progression, it also provides a threshold to get released and finally gives a platform for the V chord to provide a relaxation route to go towards the first (i) chord again.

The aesthetics involved with chords does basically come out with their use on instruments in a progressive manner, either with or without rhythm. Even the same chord progression may give different impressions at different times because of the instrumentation, playing techniques, and/or other musical variants. It is all about experimentation and having a firm plan about the usage of chords, which reflects the aesthetics of a composer.

I have gathered and researched several views about the mood and emotions associated with notes. In Indian classical music, there are so many ragas which have all the natural notes and these compositions reflect different moods, like sharp, soft and normal. In these ragas, the *chalan* (a peculiar pattern of using the notes) decides the mood. Any two *ragas* with the same notes with different peculiar patterns of using the notes may reflect two different moods. So, it may not be necessarily true in all cases of music that sharp or flat notes contribute in emotion and mood-building. It is the pattern of using notes with style of delivering it through sound and its dynamics which contributes to the production and enhancement of the mood and emotion.

Sir James Jeans believes that the role of every additional sharp in the key signature is to add to the brightness and sparkle of the music, while every flat should contribute to softness, pensiveness, and even melancholy.[12]

Several musicians have shared with me their thoughts regarding the characteristics and moods of notes. I believe these kinds of thoughts are very much personalised and are not of universal acceptance.

As far as the aesthetics of chords is concerned, all the musical elements are associated with presentation like playing, voicing, orchestration, harmonisation, etc. Along with usage of chords with modes, scales and chord progressions—in all possible manners—helps enhance the expressiveness of a composition.

USAGES OF CHORDS AND HARMONY IN INDIAN FILM MUSIC

Music has been an integral part of Indian cinema from the time sound was introduced in films. As the orchestration developed, the size of the orchestra used in films also grew. In the initial years, film orchestras only included a few instruments like harmonium, violin, tabla etc. But later, in the later 40s, it grew from 10-20 instruments to 20-30 instruments. Some composers even started using additional instruments, especially group violins, using as many as a hundred of them. The increase in size of the orchestra led to the use of techniques of western music. If we listen to the early music of Indian films, the entire orchestra was used in unison with vocals, and even in interludes. As orchestration techniques got incorporated later, the elements of western music like harmony, chords etc. were introduced. Naushad, O. P. Nayyar, Shankar-Jaikishan were among the music directors who used large orchestras. Naushad used orchestra in Indian music style. Shankar-Jaikishan, O. P. Nayyar and Salil Chaudhry were the ones who introduced western elements of

---

[12] Jeans, Sir James. Science & Music. Cambridge University Press, 1961, p.182

music to Indian cinema. Their compositions blended different styles of world and they also used very rich orchestration.

Till the mid 60's, music compositions were mostly based on ragas, and were almost based on modal melodic movements. Unlike in western music, our film compositions back then used both the 3rd notes (flat and perfect), both the 4th notes (perfect and sharp) and both 7th notes (flat and perfect) in one or different compositions. Some compositions were also made on harmonic movements, but that was only seen occasionally. In spite of the harmonic movement in compositions, composers used tonal variation from different parts of the world, especially Persian music.

It is argued that till that time, the songs were basically based on *ragas* not in harmonic movement, though some composers like Shankar Jaikishan, O. P. Nayyar, Salil Chaudhary, and R. D. Burman had started their working based on harmonic movements. However, it was not used in a dominating way, but they reflected their keen interest towards harmonic movements.

IMAGE 1 (Famous playback singer Sharda Rajan with musicians)

Actually, it is because of the uniqueness of Indian film music and Indian tradition that there may be accompaniment of either melodic or harmonic or both styles. It is almost true that till the mid 1990s, the usage of chords in terms of variety was normally limited to major and minor triads. Other types of chords like seventh, diminished, suspended, sixth etc. were rarely used till the mid-1990s. R. D. Burman's creations can be excluded from the list because he heavily used electronic instruments and, of course, different types of chords.

After electronic music became mainstream in Indian films, it changed the scenario of film music regarding the use of chords. In the time of A. R Rahman, Jatin-Lalit and later Pritam, Salim-Sulaiman, Shankar-Ehsaan-Loy, Vishal-Shekhar, etc. the broad spectrum of chords has been taken in use, especially with the elements of electronic sound. Actually till the 1990s, harmonisation was secondary for the composer, though their musical teams did try to have it whenever possible.

From the mid-1990s, in Indian film music, melodies were widely composed in harmonic progressions. Other elements like arpeggios, cadences and variety of chords also came into mainstream usage. However, it is not true that no one had used these elements before. Though it was rare, music directors like R. D. Burman, Laxmikant Pyarelal, Kalyanji-Anandji, Salil Chaudhary and a few other composers in the earlier times used these elements in their compositions, preludes and interludes. Shiv-Hari used very strong harmonic progressions with chords and orchestration in their song *'Ye Kahan Aa Gaye Hum'* in the movie *Silsila*; the prelude of this song is very aggressive on the harmonic line. They also used the whole tone scale in this song at a point in prelude. This song was arranged by music arranger Kishore Sharma. During the course of writing this book, I got the chance to interview him when he spoke about this song. He said, "I started the introductory music with a diminished chord and made runs of strings from this chord. After making so many phrases, the music comes downward through a sequence of whole tone scale. This is one of my favourite songs."

R. D. Burman composed songs like '*Jab Chaha Yaara Tumne*' (in the movie, *Zabardast*), 'Kiski Sadayen' (*Red Rose*), and '*Ana Re Ana Re*' (*Gurudev*) in rare harmonic progressions. He used arpeggios in many songs, including the popular number "*Dil Lena Khel Hai Dildar Ka*". Salil Chaudhary has also shown his mastery in harmonic progressions in songs like '*Baag Mein Kali Khili*'. He was very keen on harmonising, especially in his interludes, and sometimes rare progression in melodies, too. Hemant Kumar, and Shankar-Jaikishan made the best blend of Indian and western musical elements in their time.

The drive to use bigger orchestras has come to existence due to innovative ideas coming in the working of music composers. Later on it became a trend in Indian cinema. The change of use of technologies in the part of orchestration as well as recordings was obvious progress in the cinematic music of India. "Large scale orchestral accompaniments first appeared in particularly large budget or epic films of the 1950s, such as Awara (1951), Aan (1952) and Mother India (1957) and later became the norm."[13] The time period between 1950 to 1960 was literally important as it gave composers and producers a clearer idea of usage of bigger orchestra.

When the practices and elements of western music were being introduced, it started from unison-playing, then two-part harmonies, and then complex harmonies, which is quite usual. So, the Indian film music developed naturally. Nowadays, chords, sequences and harmonies are liberally used to make film music.

Some songs with rare chord progressions, according to my understanding, are:

---

[13] Morcom, Anna. Hindi Film Songs and Cinema. Ashghate, 2007, p.86

1. Baag Me Kali Khili (Chand Aur Suraj)
2. Ae Ajnabi (Baaz)
3. Bazigar O Bazigar (Bazigar)
4. Jab Chaha Yaara Tumne (Zabardast)
5. Kiski Sadayen Mujhko Bulayen (Red Rose)
6. Sanwre (Bandit Queen)
7. Huzoor-E-Wala (Ye Raat Phir Na Aayegi)
8. Aa Ab Laut Chalen (Jis Desh Mein Ganga Behti Hai)
9. Inteha Ho Gayi (Sharabi)
10. Na Jiya Lage Na (Anand)
11. Bheegi Bheegi Raaton Mein (Ajnabee)
12. Roop Tera Mastana (Aradhna)
13. Aaja Aaja Main Hun Pyar Tera (Teesri Manzil)
14. Dil Ke Jharokhe Me (Bramhachari)
15. Lekar Hum Deewana Dil (Yaadon Ki Barat)

Here is a table about the chords for the music of the 2nd interlude of a song from the film, *Shaan*.

(Yamma Yamma—Shaan, IInd music origins from B^m. Key of Song- A major)

Bm	Em/Em7/A	D	Am/F#/F#7/A#dim7	B^m	E^m	D	D
B♭	G#	B♭	G#	Em	A7	A7	A

Another good example for good harmonic chord progression is from the film *Lekin*:

(Surmai Shaam, IInd music origins from G9-Lekin, Key of Song- G major)

G9	G9	G9	G9	G	G	Bm	Bm
G	G	Cm	Cm	Cm	Cm	G	G
Cm	G	G	G	G	G	D7	D7
D7	D7	G	D	G	G	G	G

STUDY OF CHORDS & ITS AESTHETICS –

(In Compositions & Orchestration of Prominent Indian Film Composers)

To study chords and its aesthetics in Indian film music, it is a tough task to decide which composers should be considered for discussion. Till the 1980s itself, Indian films had seen the work of several immensely talented music directors like Gulam Haider, Jaidev, Anil Vishwas, Khemchand Prakash, Pankaj Malik, Hemant Kumar, Shankar Jaikishan, S.D. Burman, R.D. Burman, Laxmikant Pyarelal, Salil Choudhary, Roshan, Chitragupt, Kalyanji Anandji, Madan Mohan, C. Ramchandra, Husn Lal Bhagat Ram, Naushad, O.P. Nayyar, Sonik Omi, Ravindra Jain, Rajesh Roshan, Bappi Lahiri, Usha Khanna, Hriday Nath Mangeshkar, Shiv Hari, Khayyam, Illaiyaraja, Ravi, Uttam Singh, and Ram Laxman.

The following decades till now saw fresh music directors rise to the top, including Anu Malik, Anand Milind, Nadeem Sharvan, Jatin Lalit, Dilip Sen Sameer Sen, A.R. Rahman, Adesh Shrivastava, Nikhil Vinay, Sajid Wajid, Shantanu Moitra, Ismail Darbar, Shankar Ehsan Loy, M.M. Kreem, Pritam, Salim Sulaiman, Himesh Reshammiya, Vishal Bharadwaj, Vishal Shekhar, and Jeet Ganguly among others. Many of the above names are still working in the film industry.

As discussed in the previous section, orchestration in the film industry underwent various changes, from unison-playing to bi-parted harmonic-playing, and evolved even beyond that. Earlier, music directors were not very keen on playing chords and their progressions. However, somewhere around the mid 1950s, the interest towards chords and harmonies began to develop, and later on, it came into use for film sound. The orchestration with all western music techniques was introduced; O.P. Nayyar and Shankar Jaikishan were among the first ones to use it widely. Normally this usage was limited to just the simple major and minor scale. Two-part harmonies were used on the string segments. Strumming of guitar was also used that time.

Some experimental composers like Shankar-Jaikishan, O.P. Nayyar, R.D. Burman, Salil Chaudhary and Laxmikant Pyarelal were keen on enriching the orchestration with western elements. Around the 1970s, little complex chords and their progressions were introduced, apart from regular major and minor scale progressions. In the song *'Dil Ke Jharokhe Mein Tujhko Bithake'* from the film *'Bramhachari'*, Shankar-Jaikishan used the sixth chord in the progression. S.D. Burman used the dominant seventh chord too prominently in the song *'Roop Tera Mastana'* from the film, *'Aaradhna'*.

Though O.P. Nayyar worked in regular progressions, the heavy usage of chromatic notes in vocals and lead instruments was his peculiarity which made his work stand out. Later on, R.D. Burman came into the limelight because of his vast and experimental musical structures, starting from his big break, *'Teesri Manzil'*. He used different tones in instrumentation as well as kicked off many trends by using of western music elements. He used bass guitar prominently in his soundtracks. In his career, he also used electronic instruments, and different kinds of rhythm patterns with a blend of cross and off beats in Latin and Indian rhythm. Arpeggio is also an element which was probably used for the first time in Indian film music by R.D. Burman.

Salil Chaudhary was another great composer who worked a lot on western elements along with the blend of Indian melodic structures. Remember the prelude of his song *'Jago Mohan Pyare'* from the film, *'Jaagte Raho'*. This song set a new trend of prelude with choir in harmonic progression. The same kind of music was created by Shankar Jaikishan in *'O Basanti Pawan Pagal'* from *'Jis Desh Mein Ganga Behti Hai'*. *'Bagh Me Kali Khili'* from the film *'Chand Aur Suraj'* composed by Salil Chaudhary is another example of his obsession with harmonic progressions. He also used arpeggiation technique in several compositions like *'Rajnigandha Phool Tumhare Yun Hi Mehke Jeevan Mein'* from the film, *'Rajnigandha'*. Laxmikant and Pyarelal were the only composers at their time who arranged music on their own (Pyarelal Sharma is himself well-versed with western and Indian music). Some peculiar songs of this duo are *Dream Girl* (*Dream Girl*), *Suno Sajna Papihe Ne* (*Aaye Din Bahar Ke*), and *Aate Jaate Khubsurat Awara Sadkon Pe* (*Anurodh*) in which conventional and experimental works can be easily seen. Another song that deserves to be mentioned is *'Roz Sham Aati Thi'* from the film *'Imtihaan'*, in which different kinds of chromatics were used with punchy bassline and nice chord progression.

Since the 1970s, composers have been taking serious effort to use complex chord progression in orchestration and sometimes in tunes, too. This has given us many unique songs. Especially from the mid-90s, the aesthetics towards chords and orchestration saw a 180-degree change as far as the usage and presentation is concerned in the Indian film songs. Music directors like Jatin-Lalit, A.R. Rahman, Ismail Darbar, Vishal-Shekhar, Shankar Ehsan Loy, Pritam, Salim-Sulaiman, Vishal Bharadwaj, Himesh Reshammiya and many more who are still working today, contributed towards the change of Indian cinematic music as far as aesthetic vision for chords and orchestration is concerned.

Chapter 3

Tune Making & Aesthetics

"The choice of chords to be used totally depends on the type of music you are composing. When we work on hardcore Indian classical music, we work with limitations of the music and cannot use many chords. But when we have the liberty, we can do what we want."

–Sunil Kaushik

What is Tune

There are several opinions regarding the definitions of tune, or melody. Tune and melody are sometimes used as synonyms, while other times, they are seen as two different terms. We will discuss these terms in light of musical structure or composition. When someone is heard to be singing well, then one might say, "He is singing a nice melody." And when an instrumentalist plays something nice in the lead, then one would normally say, "He is playing a nice tune". These statements are common. It's all about perception and understanding. In Indian music industry, a tune is generally referred to as an overall music composition in Indian music industry. It is a big musical structure. In the broader way, we can say that a tune is a combination of multiple melodies or a combination of melodies and harmonies.

In Indian film music terminology, the tune is a series of various melodic structures. It may involve harmonies and orchestration, too. Usually, 'melody' can mean 'linear sequences of suited tones'. I have noticed that melody is often called as the antonym of harmony; we can say the tune is a combination of both. Melody is the basic part of a tune; I call it the spinal cord of a tune. So, tune is a broader term in lieu of melody. Sometimes, 'tune' is also used for a solo piece of an instrument. Melody and harmony are not separable parts, as Arnold Schoenberg said, "The composer should never invent a melody without being conscious of its harmony."[14]

---

[14] Schoenberg, Arnold. Fundamentals and Musical Composition. Faber and Faber Limited, 1967, p.3.

As a whole, a tune itself is a complete story of melodies, and harmonies are its sentences. Though these musical sentences are complete in nature, the thought behind the tune sees success when these sentences properly connect as a theme. Without the emergence of a meaningful and beautiful interpretation, it wouldn't be a tune but only a cluster. This cluster may be meaningful as a musical structure, but may not be as a tune or a composition.

Perfect Tune

'Perfect tune' is a relative term. Achieving perfection in composition and musical language is a continuous process. With time, many thoughts regarding successful musical structures have changed or modified. New thoughts and doctrines have also come into existence. For every new composition, a new composer makes new and different blends of old and new forms of music to get a unique result. It is like making different structures each time with the same raw material.

Music educator Margaret Lucy Wilkins believes that famous Spanish architect Antoni Gaudi's (1852-1926) approach to planning could be a model for composers. "The Gaudi model provides a good balance between complete control over every facet of the construction and the opportunity to allow creative inspiration to adorn the basic structure," she wrote in 2006.[15] Gaudi worked by supplying basic architectural plans and then intuitively suggested ideas as the construction of the structure progressed. In music composition, composers should take structural planning as part of the process while striving to achieve this balance between control and creativity.

A better way to make a 'perfect tune' is to judge your musical structure. Though it is very tough, better aesthetics and

---

[15] Wilkins, Margaret. Creative Music Composition: The Young Composer's Voice. Taylor & Francis, 2006, p.24.

a good teacher may help one judge the perfection level from the audience's perception. To make a perfect tune, a composer might need to experiment with a few styles for the desired musical expression. The nature of the composer's inclination towards definite styles of music and their structures will lead him to achieve perfection as per his musical knowledge and experience. This may help him in perfecting both his style and tune.

A perfect tune is somewhat a musical structure which fulfils the composer's as well as the listener's aesthetic thirst. Because aesthetic thirst towards any aesthetic form leads the creation according to the aesthetic goal, the perfection comes with an end product as per the level of knowledge and experience of the artist.

One can study and analyse various schools of thought which came into existence regarding creation of musical structures in order to reach the perfection level. The schools of thought summarised by Margaret Luci Wilkins in the book *Creative Music Composition* are: Twelve Tone Technique by Arnold Shoenberg, Microtonality by Iannis Xenakis and Giacinto Scelsi, Post Modernism by Henryk Gorecki, Minimalism by Steve Reich, John Adams, Louis Andreissen, Sonic Compositions by Rebbecca Sounders, Gesture by Sofia Gubaidulina, Experimental By John Cage and Pauline Oliveros, Avante Garde by Pierre Boulez and Karlheinz Stockhousen, Post Serialism by Harrison Birtwistle, The New Tonality by Judith Weir, Polystylicity by Alfred Schnittke, Spectralism by Tristan Murail and Livia Teodorescn, Specialisation by Thea Musgrave, and New Complexity by Brian Ferneyhough.

Twelve-Tone Technique was the idea propagated by Arnold Shoenberg. He arranged all the twelve chromatic notes in a row as the unique scale or mode. These twelve notes were used only once in a row. Then the whole composition was designed from that row and its variants. This kind of unique experiment allows a composer to create the perfect tune as per his aesthetic directives. Hence, a composer should be experimental, knowledgeable, and of course a good learner of new ideas.

Types of Tunes and Musical Structures

When we talk about world music, an indefinite number of musical structures seem to be in existence. They may be distinctive in style or versions or at any extent. Hence, it is very difficult to speak about all the types of tunes, melodies or musical structures. People aware about western music are also often familiar with the terms: sonata, concerto, symphony, etc. There are also genres which basically denote the kind of musical form or structural construct they follow. Some are named after the rhythm form like adagio, allegro etc. In Indian music, there are so many kinds of structures present in tradition, whether it is classical, light or folk music.

In Indian classical music, Dhrupad, Khayal, Tarana, Tappa etc. are the types of musical structures. Folk music has a lot of variations with respect to the structural construct. Each form of folk music has its own peculiarities. The folk music forms in India include Biraha (Baghelkhand), Lavani (Maharashtra), Beehu (Assam), Ghoomar (Rajasthan), Giddha (Punjab), Chaiti (Uttar Pradesh), and Bhawai (Gujarat). They have a long list in terms of musical structures. Light and semi-classical music of India also have the same situation. Ghazal, Geet, Nagma, Qawwali, Bhajan, Thumri, Dadra, etc. come under this category.

In the world of music, Indian film music is now seen as a separate segment with categories such as romantic, sad, club songs, cabaret, mujra etc. When a producer or director approaches a music composer, he simply specifies that the tune should be for club songs, or mujra, or as the film's requirement. More than that, music composers are also briefed about the style and genre for certain tracks. The most important fact is that all these types of tunes, melodies or musical structures are the results of different views and approaches related to aesthetic senses of different people, cultures and ethnicities.

THOUGHT PROCESS OF MAKING A TUNE

The making of a tune is certainly administered by thought process. This thought process may differ from person to person. In my opinion, there is a psycho-imaging process through which a composer makes a musical image of his thoughts about a song whether it is lyrical or instrumental. This thought process gets completed in these steps:

- A. Perception building
- B. Making a theme
- C. Developing a theme to a musical structure
- D. Reaching on a perfect tune
- E. Testing for acceptance
- F. Presentation design of a tune

These are six basic steps for the thought process of making a tune. Now, even though we will discuss the making of a tune in terms of Indian film music production, the basic efforts should work for any song or tune.

Composing a song is a work of art in which the lyrics are made colourful by adding musical elements of expression. It depends on the aesthetics of the composer. To get the right emotional expression, the composer should be clear about the theme of the song. Then, according to the theme, the composer can come up with an emotional and sensible base in his conscious mind. After this, he should conceptualise the basic structure of the tune or melody. This conceptualisation is followed by the selection of rhythm pattern and grooves, keynote, chord sequence and progression, orchestration, harmonisation and reharmonisation, singing pattern and style. And after this, the composer will have a perfect tune as per his aesthetics and the needs of the film. This perfect tune will then be tested for acceptance among some people, either commercial trade experts of music, or a select group of people representing the existing market. A team of production members—which may comprise a film director, lyricist, producer, composer and some important people behind the film—usually holds a discussion on the composed song as a perfect tune. Some creative input from the discussion can be added to the tune as per the needs of film and lyrics. After these actions, the tune goes to the designing part for the final presentation. This gets concluded with sound programming and music arrangement, acoustic dubbing, dubbing of vocal and chorus, final mixing and mastering.

Each step involved in this process contributes in making the tune better, and the final song is prepared to release for the audience. Now we will discuss these steps briefly.

A. Perception Building

To create a composition based on lyrics, it's very important to analyse the theme, emotional posture, rhyming and meter, and internal and external flow or tempo of the mood in the lyrics. Understanding the scenarios of the lyrics and variations of emotions is very critical. The composer must understand the interpretations of words and emotions because this is when the seed of the hypothetical concept of tune sprouts in his mind. Interpreting the internal current of mood in the lines of the song is a little difficult and critical, too, in terms of the perception of the tune. Perception does not have a physical appearance, so the psycho-analytical process enables one to visualise it in a musical and physical form. Perception building is just like looking for a needle in a haystack, it is the search for the base of a concept. When a composer completes his journey finalising the lyrics and its content, he moves on to build a perception for the tune.

B. MAKING A THEME

After understanding the content and building the perception, creating a theme is an important step towards getting a tune. This theme is created by preparing an emotional and sensible base. The base depends on the individuality of the composer.

We can say that this unique, emotional and sensible base is a result of the speciality of the composer's earned individuality. For making a theme, the composer studies the situation and storyline of the song, relations of different characters in the story and how the song will come in place of actual dialogues. He feels the emotional status of the song by his biological and psychological impulses and also feels the mood.

The composer connects his sensitive side with the song and feels an emotional scene inside his mind, depending on his prior experiences. This gives him an urge related to the musical structure. This drive is the seed of tune or melody, or you can say that this is a hypothetical concept of tune which comes out as a basic musical structure.

This base is an extreme result of experience and expertise of the composer. This experience is related to all aspects of life, whether musical or not. That is why, from the broad experience of life, music also keeps getting better over time. The feeling of sensitivity drives one to come up with a rich musical structure. The theme for the tune is the first musical expression for the song and this theme works as a base for all other musical elements of expression of emotion and mood. This is the transcription of that urge into a musical structure. After getting this theme, maximum elements are functionalised on the basis of technique, skill, experience and aesthetic sense. Hence, getting the theme and accomplishment of tune is totally a musical psychoanalytical aesthetic process.

C. DEVELOPING THE THEME TO A MUSICAL STRUCTURE

The composer develops the theme of the tune into a complete musical structure through the different technical aspects. In this step, colouring of words, emotions and musical phrases is done with the help of these technical activities. It involves not only the musical skills and experiences of the composer, but also his whole life experience, whether it is of social, economical, political, cultural life or spiritual, psychological, academic or traditional life. Many factors of sound physics are also included in this process.

In my opinion, the elements which contribute to the development of the theme can also be named as the 'elements of denotation of musical expression of a song'. These elements are:

1. Melody or Tune
2. Rhythm section
3. Selection of key note
4. Harmonisation and chord progression
5. Orchestration arrangement techniques
6. Enhancement of mood through specialities of singing and instruments
7. Balance

1. MELODY OR TUNE

Making a tune from the very beginning is a very personal and unique job. In this process, rules are followed in the lowest magnitude because the impulses for a tune do not come out in a predefined pattern. Different dimensions of tune start coming to the thoughts of the composer as he goes through the content of the song. When I study the lyrics, I start getting ideas about the style of tune, format, flow of notes, pattern of intervals between notes, symmetry of notes, descendo and crescendo of notes, and harmonic patterns. The basic structure of the tune gets finalised after completing the theme preparation. This could take a few seconds in some cases, but can also take several days or even months.

There are many factors which are responsible for the creation of melody and its structural construct. The ascending and descending movements of notes are important as the elements of the melody being created. The key scale, on which the melody is being formed and created, plays a vital role because the basic notes of any scale provides the platform to develop a melodic thought in the shape of music. Furthermore, the experimentation with the notes of selected scale—may be either by blending with any other scale or altering semitones— gives an open field to come up with a sharper or brighter melodic movement. Composers use many musical tools to get variations from the basic tune, like skipping, adding or repeating notes from the same scale chosen for the first thought of the tune. They may also explore other scales. These tricks depend on the use of different intervals and patterns of notes. In Indian music, there are many *ragas* which have been blended so beautifully in the melodic structures. The song '*Bandhan Toote Na*' is a great example of Laxmikant-Pyarelal's blending techniques and experimentation, from the film '*Mom Ki Gudiya*'. In this song, the scale has the flat 2nd note in accordance with a particular raga but the composer also used perfect 2nd very prominently in the same small melodic phrase. This shows that intervallic experimentation is helpful in getting a nice melodic structure.

Apart from going for semitonic alteration, a composer can change the dynamics of notes. Increasing or decreasing the magnitudes in dynamics of notes may put on different colours and feel in the melody. Playing techniques of different instruments like staccato and legato to get different types of articulations with dynamics may also be helpful. This is the basic idea on the basis of which the melody can be analysed and developed. A competent composer has all the tools in his bag required to bang the target. His knowledge, exposure and experience lead his experimentation to the level where he will always achieve a result that will fulfil his musical needs. A skillful and smart balance between the experiments with techniques, traditions, and ideas always works to achieve fine musical statements.

2. RHYTHM SECTION

After analysing melody, it is necessary to take on the rhythm section. Deciding the frame of rhythm and selection of particular groove and style is very important because a wrong selection may ruin the mood and effect of the tune. Be it simple rhythm or complex rhythm pattern, selecting according to the need of tune and aesthetics is a major decision that will affect the beauty of tune. After this, the composer has to decide the tempo of the song.

3. SELECTION OF KEY NOTE

After developing the rhythm section, the composer selects the key note of the tune for a particular recording or presentation. In reference to Indian classical music, it is called the selection of Sa (Shadaj). The key note is the basic note from where the key signature is assigned and all the notations are made. All other elements of musical expression can only be functionalized after selection of this key note. The basic idea behind selecting an appropriate key note is to make the best sound design of the tune for maximised expressions and effects.

Intensity and pitch of sound for any tune is important because lower or higher key notes may affect the tune adversely in terms of beauty and expression. For a better selection of key notes, a composer should estimate and judge the capacity and quality of the singer. The instrument which may be used for the tune's orchestration should be evaluated, too. It is all about the expertise and wisdom of the composer, otherwise the vocal quality and timber quality of instruments would not be capitalised properly. The selection of tonic chords is also done simultaneously.

4. HARMONISATION AND CHORD PROGRESSION

Harmony is an element which adds glitter in accordance with the tune. It is also capable of changing the mood of the tune. This is because, apart from being relevant to the melody, harmony is equally present as melody. It is better to plan out a harmony instead of creating it in haste. Some harmonies come along with the tune but if it is done in a planned way, the harmony becomes more powerful and effective in terms of expression. There are three major steps in the process of harmonisation: melodic analysis, bass melody creation, and chord selection.

In melodic analysis, the composer evaluates the specialities of the tune. In this process, the composer examines trichords, overall consonant, skips and symmetry, etc. It means, according to Indian music, the harmony for a tune is designed on the basis of *alpatva-bahutva* (alpatva i.e. using any note in minimum way; *bahutva* i.e. using any note in maximum way), *langhan* (skipping any note in a certain way in ascending or descending, or both orders), *vaad-samvaad* (dialogue between notes), and *swar-yugm* (pair of two notes). The design of harmony gets matured by keeping the following points in mind:

- Emotional aspects
- Peculiarity of style
- Cadence point (phrases produced by ascending and descending tonal inflection from tone)
- Factors related to balance of note
- Point of climax (the part of tune where its effectiveness is on peak and from where it returns to start point)

Hence, the composer moves towards the completion of the harmony design process according to the aesthetic senses to create an environment for the most beautiful musical mood of the tune.

In bass melody creation, the composer makes a base of tune which plays a pivotal role in the making of the whole harmony. Many musical dimensions for a tune are explored by bass melody. During the creation of bass melody, symmetry and asymmetry of intervallic patterns of notes, direction (ascending and descending series of notes in reference to original tune) by which counter points are made etc. are kept in mind. Apart from these, slow and fast notes, sustained notes, reposition, transition, cadence, relative speed with tune i.e. rhythmic strokes of notes or chords, are some factors which enhance the rhythmic beauty and also maximises expressions of tune through rhythm.

In chord selection and chord progression, a root chord has to be established by the composer as per the tonality of the tune. Along with this selection, all other chords are also selected according to the tune which makes a chord progression. Sometimes, there are some parts in a tune where many chords can be used in a single place. In this situation, the composer should select the appropriate chord accordingly so that the expressions can be enhanced. Sometimes, a sustained note comes in the tune for a while. In that place, the composer may put a small progression of all the alternative chords. For example, we can go through a part of a song from the film, *Padosan*, on E major:

> *Kehna hai, kehna hai aaj tumse ye pehli baar,*
> *Tum hi to layi ho jeevan me mere pyar pyar pyar.*

In this *mukhda*, the second line has a sustained note E in "*Tum hi to layi ho jeevan me*". The composer of this song, R. D. Burman, made a progression of three alternative chords for that sustained note E. He used three bangs of three different chords containing E note according to the tune along with its counter harmony. The chords are:

Tum hi to	Layi ho	Jeevan me	Mere
X	X	X	X
E	D♭m	A	D

The listener can feel a transit of mood in a deeper way at this motific point of the song. Similar work of using alternative chords was done by Mahesh-Kishore in the second interlude of the song *'Be-irada Nazar Mil Gayi to'* from the film *'Sanam Bewafa'*, where three alternative chords were used on a single sustained note. These examples show that the selection of chords in progression is an important activity which has to be done very carefully and creatively to enhance the beauty and expression of moods and emotion.

5. ORCHESTRATION ARRANGEMENT TECHNIQUES

In this step, the composer distributes the parts of harmony and melody for different segments of instruments and vocals. During this process, moods and expressions are treated on special priority so that the instruments can be selected according to their appropriate pitch and mood. Timbre is the quality of instruments which strongly suggests their best pitch according to sound and tune, too. In this process, decisions are made regarding making harmony light or dark in some places, stylisation of harmony, best utilisation of form and timbre of sound, and modulations, so that expressions can be made more effective.

Reharmonisation of tune is also done at the time of orchestration. For the reharmonisation of a tune, alternative chords, added note chords, accidental chords and notes, coloured notes, and chord voicings are used very frequently along with other tools and orchestration arrangement techniques. Different types of chords and their inversions, harmonic progressions, modes etc. are used to enhance the colourfulness of the tune. The climax of the tune is also made more musical to reach the extreme of beauty.

6. ENHANCEMENT OF MOOD THROUGH SPECIALITIES OF SINGING AND INSTRUMENTS

In Indian film music, singing is an important element in a song because the music is almost always situational. After orchestration, intense work is done for articulation, dynamics, effects, breathing cues, etc. of the vocals and different instruments. This is done so that the intensity of emotional expression gets enhanced. There are many elements which help enhance minute aspects of mood and emotion, like lighter or stronger stroke of guitar on a particular note, breaking a beat in many parts and ascending or descending patterns of amount of sound on a particular instrument or vocal, vocal singing techniques viz. Gamak, Murki, Khatka etc., breathing techniques, instrumental specialities viz. Krantan of Sarod or Sitar, bowing techniques of violin, and playing flute with or without jawari.

7. BALANCE

Here, the composer analyses all the elements used for the expression. With this analysis, the composer determines the exact magnitude and intensity of utility and usage of these elements according to his aesthetic view. He balances all these elements so that the effectiveness of the tune reaches a higher level. He makes sure that there is no deviation or disturbance by which the process of feeling of mood and emotion for a listener may get distracted or blocked or decreased. By doing this analysis, these elements are rectified and re-established as per common aesthetic sense of a common listener. By bringing balance, the emotional level of the tune can be determined.

D. REACHING ON A PERFECT TUNE

Following all the steps discussed so far, the composer makes a decision on the tune: whether it is perfect as per his perception and according to his aesthetic sense. Finding the perfect tune or composition is all about the artistic skills of a composer. Though this perfect tune may be dealt with further suggestions when it goes for testing of acceptance, this step still completes the thought process of making a tune.

E. TESTING FOR ACCEPTANCE

When a tune is made for a film production, this step is included sometimes to assess the effectiveness of that tune according to the film situations, market traits, stylisation, etc. The group of production members which may discuss the tune comprises film producer, director, lyricist, distributors, critics and other members, as per need and design of the production team. This team makes an assessment regarding the needed success ratio. Sometimes, the tune is exposed to common people who are also the actual target audience of the tune and their reaction is noted to see acceptability among the masses. These practices are necessary to assess acceptability, and some adjustments or changes may be done in the tune because of this step.

F. PRESENTATION DESIGN OF A TUNE

After testing for acceptance, the changes are accommodated in the tune and then the presentation design is prepared. In this process, all the production activities are done, like selection of artists for vocals and instrumentals, artist management, studios selection and administration, recording sessions, mixing and mastering for as per as the film song production is associated. For concerts, this process is done according to live performances.

This is how a tune or composition is made and produced for film. Some composers may disagree about these steps, but I strongly believe that these are the core steps which should help a composer achieve valuable results.

VIEWS AND CRITICS ON THE TUNE MAKING PROCESS AND MUSIC PRODUCTION

In the earlier sections, I have talked about the thought process that takes place in the mind of a composer during tunemaking. I discussed my views on this 'thought process' phenomenon with a few musicians and received positive responses. A few of them told me about the usual technical practice to make a plot for a tune, like the random playing of progressions or ragas. But, by doing so, they were unknowingly accepting the perceptual process.

On film music composition, all of them agreed to accept 'situation' as the base used while working on the tune. As far as the perceptual process is concerned, the tune making always involves the steps that I discussed before (perception building, making a theme, developing a theme to a musical structure, reaching on a perfect tune, testing for acceptance, and presentation design of a tune).

For perception building, 'situation' is used as a catalyst to induce and direct the perception towards the desired outcome. Every step contributes towards the betterment of the tune. The process I proposed is oriented towards moods and expression either for lyrics or music itself and certainly deals with aspects of 'situation'.

To know about different aspects of the tune-making process and music production in the Mumbai film industry, I spoke to veteran musicians Amar Haldipur, Kersi Lord, Burjor Lord, Kishore Sharma, Ashok Jagtap, Sunil Kaushik, and Merlin Desouza. Here are some important outcomes in the form of interviews and notes.

"A song should never look naked in arrangement"
- Amar Haldipur

I interviewed renowned music composer and arranger of Bollywood Amar Haldipur and veteran musician Kersi Lord in Mumbai on 18 September 2014. Haldipur expressed his views regarding tunemaking and all aspects of music production in Mumbai film Industry during the interview. The interview was based on subjects like harmony and its aesthetics and usage in film music, his experience of the industry, and views regarding music composition and orchestration. Haldipur accompanied Laxmikant-Pyarelal as a musician for decades. He was behind the music for *Shahanshah* (with Amar-Utpal). Some of his prominent works were arrangements for films like *Julie, Aur Pyar Ho Gaya,* and *Kachche Dhaage* and music albums for Ghulam Ali.

Here are the excerpts from the interview:

Abhishek Tripathi (Interviewer): Sir, what would you like to say about your learning years?

Amar Haldipur- My teacher taught me to play perfectly. He always used to say, "'See your note." When you focus your eyes on one particular object, you will never miss your notes. It is a psychological hack to make you concentrate. My teacher also helped me perfect my violin bowing. He taught me how to control my bowing through breath control.

One song of Pyare Bhai (Pyarelal) was with a time signature of 3/4. He used 5/4 and 5/8 in it, followed by 6/8 and 5/8 [Haldipur demonstrates the beats by slapping his thighs]. The initial 5/8 and the last 5/8, both were very different. It was a unique thing to learn.

Pyare Bhai's writing skills were very fast, minute and fantastic. There was no one like him in writing.

Interviewer: You are fast at writing as well. I've always admired your writing skills. I saw you several times at Sangeet studio while you were working on songs.

Haldipur: My writing is fast, but music writing requires equalization and balance. Pyare Bhai is outstanding in all aspects. I, Kishore Sharma, and thousands like me cannot stand his place. Kishore Sharma arranged music for Shiv-Hari. He was also from Pyare Bhai's school. I worked there for 33-35 years but my writing was very different. I never met anybody whose writing skills were finer than Pyare Bhai's.

Interviewer: In the song *Tu Mera Janu Hai* from the film *Hero*, the strings played in unison in the background, which was tremendous and classic. Tell me about these kinds of experiments.

Haldipur. A song should never look naked in arrangement. There must be sensible filling of instruments in the background otherwise the efforts will go in vain. Look at Sebastian's work. [Haldipur sings *Jeena Yaha marna Yaha* from the film *Mera Naam Joker*, and follows it with its counterpoint behind the vocals]. He has made incredible statements in his songs as arranger. He has done sensible filling. Nobody had ever done this before. Listen to Kersi Lord's *'Tum Jo Mil Gaye Ho'* from *Hanste Zakhm*. He used runs of violin groups from scale to scale.

I did a song for the film *'Shahenshah'* and used only major chords in the songs. *'Suno Sajna Papihe Ne'* (a song from *Aaye Din Bahar Ke*, sung by Lata Mangeshkar)— wow! What an arrangement it has. Pyare Bhai used major seventh so nicely in the whole song. Nobody is really 'creating' music. It is all in the atmosphere. Music is always re-created.

Kersi ji [also present during the interview] said that he goes to the movie theatre four times a week to learn what is good and bad in the film's music, what one needs to do and what one doesn't need to do. It's important to learn first what one does not need to do. Any chord can be good but is it useful for song? It is important to know the limitations of any implementation. An appropriate quantity of sugar makes the tea tasty, neither less nor more. A fixed quantity of the ingredients is the decisive factor of beauty of the result.

Interviewer: What is your observation about different music directors and their work?

Amar Haldipur: R .D. Burman got a boost in his career due to the youth. It's not easy to understand Laxmikant-Pyarelal's music in one stroke. 'LP' didn't get as much acceptance among the public as R. D. Burman. You can only understand LP's music if you go deep. Simple things are always easily accepted by the public. Madan Mohan ji was good in simplicity and sweetness. He had good words for songs and of course Lata Mangeshkar's incredible contribution to his songs helped. Shankar-Jaikishan's music was also great. Their songs had simple and small musical sentences. Their songs were of 4-8 bar lines, and did not generally use crosslines. [Haldipur sings *Tera Mera Pyar Amar, Phir kyun Mujhko Lagta Hai Dar*]. This is the only melody, 4 bars mukhda, and 4 bars to Stanger, and music is also of 4 bars. You should study the whole song. It is the height of using simplicity in a song.

IMAGE 2 (L to R- Renown music composer and arranger Amar Haldipur, great musician and arranger Kersi Lord and Author Abhishek Tripathi after session of discussion)

"Situation is the seed of a tune"
- Kersi Lord

Kersi Lord was a great musician, who played for the industry from 1950 till his retirement in 2000. He worked in films like *Sathi, Shalimar, Dharmatma, and Hanste Zakhm*, with music directors like Naushad, Usha Khanna, R. D. Burman, S. D. Burman, etc. He played the accordion in *'Roop Tera Mastana'* in the film *'Aradhana'*. He was the arranger for the song 'Tum Jo Mil Gaye Ho' in the film *'Hanste Zakhm'*. He spoke to me based on chords, harmonies, orchestration and arrangement, tune making, film music production and Bollywood. He passed away in 2016, leaving behind his great legacy.

These are the excerpts from the interview:

Abhishek Tripathi (Interviewer): What is a chord for a musician?

Kersi Lord: In a very simple way, melody is written horizontally and a chord is written vertically.

Interviewer: Being an arranger and musician, what is your own aesthetics about chord while making a tune or arranging for a tune?

Lord: In the present film industry, people do the melody and start the chord side-by-side, but according to me, this is not correct because the chord doesn't go with all the notes of the melody. A chord can make a different progression, different pattern altogether. When I do this, I try to do what has not been done before. I arrange the sounds differently. You can't use one formula every time.

The second-most important thing after melody is the counterpoint or what you call 'obbligato'. Sometimes obbligato also has to make some nice melody. Sometimes, if I feel I am not getting the correct obbligato due to a particular chord, I change the chord. The most important thing is nobody bothers about chord progression. You will walk with your right foot, and then the next must be left foot. You can't have two right feet. So the progression is very important. Only pianists, those who played jazz music, and jazz guitarists know the correct chord progression. People who have not studied harmonies properly won't know. The next most important thing is the bass line after melody. So progression is not as important as chords. Sometimes chords have to result in some chord only. That is called resolution of chord.

Interviewer: Which are the music directors you worked with?

Lord: From 1948 till 2000, apart from Husnlal-Bhagatram, Khemchand Prakash, and Shyam Sundar, I worked with everybody else in the industry.

Interviewer: For which music directors did you arrange music?

Lord: I first did it for Naushad Saheb. I shared a very close relation with him. I played for his background. First, he gave me a scene to write for a background. That was the training for his next film *Sathi*. He wanted a new image. If you see *Sathi*, you won't get any traditional harmony. It was different. Whenever I arranged music, I always tried to do what had never been done before.

Interviewer: When you worked with R. D. Burman or Naushad or anybody else, how did you manage to have your aesthetics in place?

Lord: Before you try out anything different, you have to discuss with the music director—things like who the actor is, what's the situation for the song, which instruments you want to use, etc. If he agrees with your idea, you can proceed further.

When I was doing background for my childhood friend Firoz Khan's *Dharmatma*, for a scene, I asked that I want to use the trumpet. It was a death scene which is why they were puzzled. I told them I will give a nice sad orchestra. I then got their permission to do it.

Actually it depends on the melody and situation. The views of the music director are also important. One should only go forward after getting their inputs.

Interviewer: What is the process of making a tune for film?

Lord: Situation is the seed of a tune. We grow our ideas on the situation. In pop albums, we don't have to think about the situation. However, film music is all about the situation.

Salil Chaudhary was fond of western classical music. Shankar-Jaikishan was oriented to the Middle East. So there was a cross country cultural mix up in music. When I did music for a play called *Tughlak*, my cousin was saying, "Kersi, are you mad? Is this music?" And The Times of India wrote, "Strange but very appropriate music by Kersi Lord."

When I was working, many people used to call me mad and after 40 years, people are giving credit to my work.

Interviewer: How do you see the development of orchestration since you started?

Kersi Lord: You are naming music directors but they used to select arrangers. If the arranger sounds different from the music director, then the result would be disastrous. Sebastian was a 'proper literate', while Anthony Gonzalves was more learned. I had played with him in the symphonies which he composed.

Sebastian was very fast. He worked for O. P. Nayyar, Shankar-Jaikishan and Salil Chaudhary. For every project, he was different. The music that he helped arrange for these three music directors seemed like they were done by three different persons. This is what a great arranger can do.

Johny Gomez has also worked very well with C Ramchandra, Chitragupt, but he showed his style everywhere.

Interviewer: Does any chord show a certain universally-accepted mood?

Lord: No, but minor chords are suitable for romantic songs. When you play a chord, the use of their inversions is also effective. If I am placing a chord in a cello, then I will place it like Sa-Pa-Ga. Ga will go in the next octave.

Because close notes in bass harmony sound woozy, I will spread it out. Close harmonies are not allowed in bass. In jazz, they use chords with different root notes also like C_m/F.

"Harmonies comes with each person in different manners"

- Sunil Kaushik

IMAGE 3 (Renown guitarist Sunil Kaushik)

Musician, composer and arranger Sunil Kaushik prominently worked as a guitarist in the 1970s. He has worked for R. D. Burman, Salil Chaudhary, Kalyanji-Anandji and other famous composers of that time. A popular song *'Neele Neele Ambar Pe Chand Jab Aaye'* has his notable contribution on the guitar. Other pioneer guitar pieces from him were in songs like *'Ek Do Teen'* (*Tezaab*), *'Tujhse Naraz Nahin Zindagi'* (*Masoom*), and *'O Sathi Re'* (*Mukaddar Ka Sikandar*). He has also scored music for animation films like Mighty Raju and Chhota Bheem.

Below are the excerpts from his interview:

Abhishek Tripathi (Interviewer): What would you say on the term 'aesthetics of chords'?

Sunil Kaushik: The choice of chords to be used totally depends on the type of music you are composing. When we work on hardcore Indian classical music, we work with limitations of the music and cannot use many chords. But when we have the liberty, we can do what we want. Like, in the song '*Waqt ne kiya kya haseen sitam*', the music part of this song is not so much related to it, but it gives a different feeling like broadness, brightness etc. In the earlier days, Salil *da* used to play with chords. His compositions were of such kind were so many chords, accidentals could be used which were not of regular use in compositions. There were different kinds of harmonies. His chord structures were so different.

Interviewer: Being an arranger and composer, somewhere in the melody line, if one or any of notes are obstructing while making a chord progression, then what do you do?

Kaushik: It all depends on what the composer thinks. Composers like Naushad or Madan Mohan worked with fixed notes. Later, R. D. Burman and the generation of composers that followed became open to experimentation. Most guitarists who compose music on guitar often change their main melody by using accidentals in due course wherever needed. So, there are no hard and fast rules for chords. Whatever suits you and sounds nice is good. The basic thing is that it should go with your melody. When I compose, it doesn't bother me if I have to change some part of the melody to get a nice harmony. It all depends on you, how much you love to use chords in the specific composition.

So, it depends on the composer, and, of course, the situation of the song. The extensions of chords are also dependent on the choice of composer. If you see a modern composer, he will never use a pure A minor chord; he may use A minor 7 normally. In one of my songs '*Rio shahar hai khushiyon ka*' from the film *Mighty Raju*, I used many extended chords. I had to come up with some bossa nova type of feel for the song. I used progression of chords like:

[CM7/ C♯dim] Am7/CM7
Dm7/F13/F11/Dm7/Dm6/B♭7/CM7/B♭7/CM7
Cross line- E♭M7/C♯M7/CM7/FM7/CM7

CM7 was tonic chords but see the cross line and see its effect. The melody is so simple but here the chord structure is giving a very different colour. In this composition, only B flat seventh is accidental normally, but I chose these chords for a different colour. It is my choice. This composition can be structured only on three chords. This is how harmonies come with each person in a different manner. You may make it simple as well as complicated based on the need and mood.

> **"Learn the rules like a professional,
> so you can break it like an artist"**
>
> - Merlin Dsouza

Jazz pianist, composer and arranger Merlin D'Souza is the daughter in law of renown music arranger Sebastian D'Souza. She arranged music in Karan Johar's *Kabhi Khushi Kabhi Gham*. Her scope of work extends to theatre, advertising, and even sonic branding. She has won several accolades like World Congress Leadership Award for Music and Rodas Women's Achievers Award.

Here are the excerpts from the interview:

Abhishek Tripathi (Interviewer): Being a composer, a pianist and a musician, how do you perceive chords when you are in the process of composing?

D'Souza: Chords are as important as a melody. The beauty of western classical music is the harmony. Bach was a mathematician, so there was mathematics in his music. Beethoven was melodic, while Chopin and Mozart were very chordal. So, chords are very important. You can portray the mood without playing a melody, and sometimes just use harmony. For example, in the film *Castaway*, when Tom Hanks

IMAGE 4 (Acclaimed jazz pianist and music arranger Merlin D'souza)

is on the island, chords are used to create a mood. Suddenly, he sees a ship coming and after a while it goes away. There are three chords used in different voicing that denote three different moods in this film.

The use of inversions of chords and their notes is very important. There may be a change of base note also. It has to be dynamic there as well. Music has to have emotions. It could be a simple chord but if it doesn't have any emotion, then it will cease the music. Even a single note can be played in different octaves with different dynamics to create a certain mood. Jumping intervals of chords may also be used.

Minor chords create expansion that is like 70mm cinema in the mind of the listener, not on the screen. If it is good to hear then it will definitely sound good on screen. It has to be a marriage of the *chords* (which are really important to create a mood), *texture*(or the melody), and *musicianship* – (important for the whole orchestra). For me, chords are very important because it is emotion. There are three things the chords can also create – melody, rhythm and harmony.

Interviewer: In isolation, does any chord denote a certain mood?

D'Souza: People usually relate minor chord with a more sad, darker feel and a major has a brighter feel but I don't think it is completely true because the most popular and hits songs of the century which have overtaken Bach and Beethoven and all jazz greats is *'Despacito'* and it is played on a minor key. So, it's the way the mood comes. Even Ed Sheeran's "*Shape of You*" is on a minor chord. A minor chord has a more romantic feel.

Interviewer: Tell me about your Bollywood experience as a musician.

D'Souza: I worked on *'Kabhi Khushi Kabhi Gham'* as the assistant music director for Sandesh Shandilya. We were working on the song – *'You are my Soniya'*, so I asked Sandesh and Karan Johar about the scene to create a chordal structure for the beginning. They told me Hrithik Roshan's character is in a London club, where he is trying to impress Kareena Kapoor's character and there are girls dancing around them. I had to compose a solo section for him. So, I wrote the lyrics and music for the same. The intro was, "you are my Soniya", so I had a chance to use all these things through my knowledge of chords and there were lots of chordal harmony with forty singers to make a nice chordal effect and Karan Johar said yes to the forty singers.

There was another song in the movie—*'Suraj Hua Maddham'*. The scene was that Shah Rukh Khan is romancing Kajol in Egypt, so I had to think about the introduction of the music. For the flashback part, I wrote an opening line and there was my voice also in that music which was followed by Alka Yagnik's voice. So, it is always important to learn classical music and its techniques. Hindustani music is more melodic; there is hardly any harmony. Thanks to Sebastian D'Souza, Chic Chocolate, and Anthony Gonsalves—they all brought the element of harmonies and orchestral jazz. It's wonderful.

Interviewer: How do you see the development of Indian film music if we divide it in three phases that is from beginning to 1970, 1970 to 1990, and 1990 onwards?

D'Souza: Indian film sound had little impact on orchestral music till around 1948. After that, harmonic effects came into picture because there was an influence of Portuguese music and all the arrangers and musicians were from Goa. There were a lot of harmonies, three-part harmony, it came after 1950. It is because at that time there was no work in Goa and they had to come to Bombay for work. So, the then music directors also wanted a fresh sound. They started to get influenced by western films. So, the scenario changed. Before that the orchestra used to play in unison only. The concept of string section was not in its original form. After the arrangers from Goa came, the sound changed because they were real composers. They started to use different harmonies, and obbligatos.

Interviewer: What is the technical difference in obligato, counterpoint and counter melody?

D'Souza: A counterpoint is three to four different melodies in eight parts. This could be many things happening at the same time, countering to come to the same conclusion.

Counter melody is two different melodies countering each other. It also has to do with harmony. Four melodies happening in the same point is the counter point which is easily and strongly seen in choirs. It's an element of mathematics, melody, harmony and rhythm. Counter melody is the melodic content with weaving. Obbligato is the filler in between the music section.

Indian arrangers have used so many beautiful obbligatos in their work and sometimes these obbligatos have been used as the main melody of songs. Look at the obbligatos of Sebastian D'Souza, who arranged vastly music for Shankar-Jaikishan, Salil Chaudhary, O. P. Nayyar.

I've named my son, Rhys Sebastian, after his grandfather. He is also a good musician who works around the globe. There was an event in Castle where performers from all over the world had come to perform. I asked him, "Rhys, what did you play there?" He said, "I played the compositions of my grandfather. I have taken compositions from his movies work like obbligatos."

Interviewer: Personally, what do you feel about the term 'aesthetics of chords'.

D'Souza: Chords are very important in delivering and enhancing the melodic content. Aesthetic of chords denotes the rightly-used chords. It is the basics. Delivering on the mood or requirement of composition of the film or media that you are composing for. It can all change. For example, if you are using A minor, we can use it with extended 9, or A minor 6th or crushed harmony like A minor 6th/minor 9th, A minor major 7th— these are used very often in jazz music. The same chords may be used with a different base note, too. For me, knowing when to flatten a note, sharpen a note, suspend a note, or augment a note is the aesthetics of chords. These are the parts of the aesthetics which I studied. It also involves tonality of inversion of notes. It is as important as mathematics to create the right aesthetics in the mind of the listener. We can also use atonality for aesthetic reasons.

To develop your aesthetics of chords, you should also practice the modes and scales. You have to learn the rules like a professional, so you can break it like an artist. It is creativity. It is very important to listen to the scales and experiment on your own.

Interviewer: When a part of a melody restricts or obstructs a more impressive chord progression, would you suggest changes in a melody if you are arranging music for someone? And what would you do if you are arranging your own composition?

D'Souza: It is my advice to everyone not to limit your creativity anywhere. Give your best wherever needed. Even as an arranger, I always look at the picture as a composer. I don't limit myself and I suggest everything for the betterment of the composition. A song becomes mine when I work on it. If I feel something wrong or to be amended, then I will ask the composer. When it comes to the question of obstruction for more impressive and beautiful chord progression, generally, I will honour the composer's melody. At the same time, I will give him an option. He should have access to my creativity and expertise. After that, it is his discretion whether he approves or rejects.

Interviewer: How do you perceive chords on psychological, physical and spiritual parameters?

Dsouza: Physical parameters are more of a technical base to deliver a certain composition. The technique comes on as a physical need to accomplish the required chordal formation. The psychological need will not be so technical as a physical need. It is more oriented towards emotional need, or—one can say—for the deliverance of mood.

"Listening to music breaks your own monotony"
- Shridhar Nagraj

IMAGE 5 (Young music composer Shirdhar Nagraj)

Mumbai-based Shridhar hails from Jabalpur and is fond of R. D. Burman. A very keen music composer working with a huge aesthetic sense of chords and harmonies, has expressed his views on request. Here is a gist of what he said at the interview:

Once while discussing music arrangements, Pyarelal ji said to me something that I will always remember. He said, "Shridhar, have you seen a painter? He does the sketching and then fills it with colour. That's the relation a composer and an arranger should have. How a bad stroke of a brush on a canvas can destroy the whole concept and aesthetic of a painting, the same applies to music-making on a mandate basis. One wrong note may be in while composing a song or its arrangements of chords can become a curse for could be cult song. And if a musician has this skill of managing both these parts efficiently, he can become a major contributor to this great subject called music."

Every composer works on the same seven or twelve notes. What makes every individual different from another is the amount of sensible and aesthetic application of the notes which actually is the perception according to me.

Every song's making has its own process and everyone has his own way. Every composer has his own sound and favorite combinations of notes. Every aspect is important.

I am fond of creating chord progressions in my crafts which have deep harmonic and melodic expression. Most of my progressions are already done while composing a melody. Even in cases where I was just involved as an arranger or a producer, the first thing which happens is the chord designing.

Chord designing is a crazy process which one cannot express in words. Many times, while listening to music, or even sometimes my own work, my constant attention is on the things happening behind the song. As a result of constant examination, I try to judge the creator's style and his take on chord growth. Perhaps, this makes it easier to break one's own monotony and make their own style. The bottom line is that listening to music is very important.

Sir Isaac Albeniz said that our brain has a balance of the conscious and the subconscious. Whatever you do, listen and read, is stored there forever, and will randomly help you at any point of life. So, listen to music as much as you can. At least it will widen your imagination which might later help you in your compositions.

DO'S AND DON'TS IN TUNE MAKING

Over the course of my career as a composer, there are certains do's and don'ts that I follow in tune making. Actually, the result of tune-making depends on the psychological, musical, and aesthetic processes that go on inside the composer. There's no trick or shortcut to find or make the best tune. It is solely an individual experience, which occurs within the composer's conscious mind. Hence, these do's and don'ts may not seem satisfactory to all.

Do's

1. Be in the best working condition and environment while making a tune.
2. Go through the details about the desired tune thoroughly, even if it is provided by the production team or yourself.
3. Deeply understand the lyrics, song and situation.
4. Educate yourself about the form of media (like radio, cinema, documentary, live concert, etc.) for which the tune is going to be made.
5. Some references regarding situation, style and other musical as well as lyrical elements may help you have a clearer vision.
6. When the first impulse of tune comes out and you go for developing its theme, just try to check the resemblance of your tune with other tunes as per your best knowledge. If the resemblance occurs, then review that part of the tune and use your skills to get out of it until it is done convincingly.
7. Test the tune regarding hummability, how it will be for common people and then make the changes accordingly.

Don'ts

1. Don't get bothered if the first impulse of tune is not coming out in a nice way. Just focus on strengthening your knowledge base.
2. If you're not getting good ideas about the details of the song, don't try to work without complete details, because it will affect the process of making tune adversely.
3. Don't get stacked with the reference material or thought because it will deviate you.

4. Don't follow just any idea unless you feel comfortable with it.
5. Don't lose focus if any resemblance occurs in your tune. Stick with the basic musical elements which you have tried while making tunes, and try more variations to match with the non-resembling part.
6. Don't fix the frame of tune until you've had the test of 'hummability'. It will make the tune more acceptable and successful.

TUNE MAKING IN INDIA

In Indian film music, the tune making process is very unique. It shows many patterns. There are many music directors who have come from different streams of Indian music. Some belong to the *gharanas* of Hindustani classical music, while some are from free segments like theatre, folk music, institutions and informal musical groups etc. Some are vocalists, whereas some are instrumentalists. Some are literate in western music, while there might be some who are untrained as well.

There have been composers whose inclination towards western music were reflected in their melodies. Some composers used Indian classical base to make tunes while using westernised orchestration. Some were stuck to Indianised orchestration along with Indianised tunes. Hence, we can say tune-making for films does not follow any definite pattern in terms of background of composers and their creations.

Many composers like Salil Chaudhary, Roshan, Kalyanji, Shankar Jaikisan, Laxmikant Pyarelal, Hemant Kumar etc., were trained in Indian classical music. Roshan and Jaidev were the disciples of Ustad Allauddin Khan (Maihar Gharana), who was a great maestro of Indian classical music. Salil Chaudhary, Hemant Kumar, and Shankar Jaikisan were among those who used Indianised melodies with a blend of westernised elements for films.

Pyarelal, Salil Chaudhary, Hemant Kumar, A. R. Rahman were well-exposed to western music also. Maximum composers of the film industry in the past were masters of one or more instruments. Shiv-Hari (duo of Pt. Shiv Kumar Sharma – Santoor, and Pt. Hari Prasad Chaurasiya – Flute) are the great maestros of Indian classical music who composed enormous soundtracks for Yash Chopra's films. Many of their tunes have unique western elements also. Pt. Ravi Shankar (sitar) and Ustad Zakir Hussain (tabla) are some other popular maestros from Indian classical music who also worked as film music composers.

There's a long list of maestros of Indian classical music who have worked as musicians for different music composers in the film industry. A famous tune (of the film, *Hero*) in the song *'Lambi Judai'* was played on the flute by Pt. Hari Prasad Chaurasiya exclusively for Laxmikant-Pyarelal. The *jugalbandi* of Pt. Shivkumar Sharma (santoor) and Ustad Rais Khan (sitar) can be called as a distinctive part of O. P. Nayyar's song, *'Jaiye Aap Kahan Jayenge'*.

A few veteran composers also had children follow their footsteps to have a successful career in the Indian film industry. R. D. Burman was the son of the great composer S. D. Burman. He worked for many blockbuster films like *Teesri Manzil, Hare Ram Hare Krishna, Karvan, Betab, Love Story, 1942—A Love Story*. Music director Rajesh Roshan is the son of the legendary composer Roshan. Some of Rajesh Roshan's noteworthy contributions were in *Kaamchor, Khudgarz, and Koyla*. Another name in this regard is Anu Malik, who is the son of music composer Sardar Malik. Anu Malik is known for composing popular tracks for several hit movies like *Aawargi, Sohni Mahiwal, Border,* and *Baazigar*. Music director duo Anand-Milind are the sons of music composer Chitragupt. Anand-Milind composed music for films like *Qayamat Se Qayamat Tak, Dil* and *Beta* etc. Even among musicians and arrangers, there are many families who have contributed to the industry for generations.

It is difficult to claim that there have been or are untrained film composers in India. However, it may be possible that a section of people entered the film music business without receiving a formal education in the field.

IMPACT OF KNOWLEDGE OF CHORDS IN MAKING AND DEVELOPING A TUNE

For a composer, the knowledge of chords is an important asset. If you are not aware of or acquainted with the system of chords, chord progressions, you will simply play the notes of that composition. Otherwise, at first, we search for a root note from where the composition is going to begin. Later on, we try to search the next note for a tune. Usually, we pick up a chord progression or a predefined chord progression or sometimes our favourite chord progressions and its improvisation.

It depends on your mental condition at that particular time. Sometimes, the case is such that your thoughts are influenced by a piece of music or chord sequences and cadences that you heard or practiced recently. So, while composing, if you have the knowledge of chords, just introduce your favourite chords after fixing the note and root chord. If I am composing on C♯ major, I can go with these progressions:

1. C♯, F♯, B♭, E♭m, C♯
2. C♯, A, B, C♯

For the second progression, you can refer to the song *"Tumse Milna, Batein Karna, Bada Achchha Lagta Hai"* (Film – *Tere Naam*; music director - Himesh Reshammiya) if the scale is C sharp major. Apart from the tonic chord (major), in this progression, all other chords come from a progression of minor chord progression. In Indian music system, this song can be called as based on *raga 'Charukeshi'*.

If you are making a chord-based or harmony-based composition for any purpose—may it be cinematic music, group song or something else—the basic composition gets simplified. Though the harmonies or the composition may be very complicated, the notes are not too entangled. A *'taan* of a *raga'* is not a harmony- or a chord-based melody. Basically, in a chord or harmony-based composition, you naturally get to compose slightly-simpler and not-so-complicated tunes. Though you can raise the emotion, essence and fragrances by accidentals, there are other factors which affect a composition positively.

A thing that is also very noticeable is that when the peculiar Indian Thumri- or Dadra-type composition is reproduced for a cinematic purpose, it comes in a simpler and easier form. I think, this simplification is done to introduce chord progressions and harmonies to that particular song and make it more acceptable, hummable, popular and understandable to even those who are not familiar with the complexities of Hindustani music systems.

If a composer has decent knowledge of the chord progression, approach chords and accidentals, he might go beyond the notes of a composition. He might use it with more musical aggression, apart from using the grains of the notes of composition only.

The word 'chord' comes from the word accordance; something which is in accordance with the tune. So, chords were basically developed or used to accompany a tune. But over time, it is likely that they might have been developed as a procedure because people sounded the chords at the first step and on the basis of chords, they must have made some good tunes.

If you go for Irish music or genres with similar styles, you can easily get a glance of the perpetual and profound effect of chords. Even in jazz or blues, it seems that the entire tune is made up on the basis of chords and traditional tune. If you go for gospel music, you'll find that most of the composition is made up on a chord progression.

When we talk about making compositions on the basis of the *raga*, the story is totally different. With the knowledge of the process of creating a chord progression, we can easily use the notes which are not coming in the *raga*. It can also be said in the way that usage of *Vivadi swar* can easily be done through the chord progressions. Strictly, it should be kept in mind that maintaining the criteria (*maryada* or limit or modesty) of that particular music style for which the tune is being composed, is a must while using chord progressions to enhance the overall impact.

In international context, most of the musical styles have their own way of using chords and harmonies. Harmony patterns of a musical style may sound dissonant to the other musical styles. For example, in blues, it sounds very stony because if they start with the seventh chord, then the entire chord progression might often have the seventh chord. If they are starting with a sixth chord, it may be full of sixth. But this is not very acceptable in Indian music patterns.

To add colour to a tune, if you are making it in Punjabi style, or some semi-classical *tappa* or *sufi* songs, it will be a good idea to introduce blues notes or chords to the tune's chord progression. It is the knowledge of chords that positively affects the process of making and developing a tune.

When you are well-versed with chords, you can introduce more than one tonic chords in a tune. By using different tonic in some part of a tune, the accidentals of that tonic will sound much-unexpected accidentals to the tune, which also can be tried to improve the overall effect of a song. This is one of the many ways to experiment with chords.

Indian Raga System versus Chord Progression System In Tune Making

Indian classical music is based on the *raga* system, which basically results in melodic structures; harmony is almost absent there. As per my knowledge, western music is based on harmonic musical structures. In the case of Indian film music, we see that it has a mixture of Indian and world music. Traces of western musical elements can be easily heard in the songs from the initial Indian films which had music.

In the tune-making, especially for Indian film music, both *raga* and chord systems are followed by the composers. A tune can be made on the basis of a *raga*-only or chord-based or blends of both. Both the systems are equally good and important. In Indian perspective, when a composer begins his work to make a tune (Indian tune), at first, he perceives a group of notes as per the need of lyrics, and at that time, he may be following the *raga* system. For example, if a song contains the mood and lyrics regarding monsoon (Saawan-Bhadon month in Indian calender) he may try the *ragas* of that season as prescribed in the Indian classical music system, like Megh, Malhar, etc.

As per my view, if a composition is being made on the basis of a *raga*, we can use the chord progression of that *raga* notes. We might find a good blend of accidental notes and chords, which will definitely enhance the beauty of the tune. Some of the composers use chord progression to make a tune and then they take inspiration from a particular *raga*, and the result is equally appealing.

So, whether a *raga*-based tune is blended with chord progressions later or a chord progression-based tune is touched by a particular *raga*, the process will yield a favourable result in aspects of beauty and ornamental patterns.

If we make a chord progression of a *raga*, it is not necessary that the notes coming in that progression will only be from the *raga* notes. In my opinion, using those notes within the tune creates a glowing canvas of tune and it certainly enhances the quality of tune.

It depends on the composer about what he opts for during the process of composing. However, this skillful blend of *ragas* and chord progressions definitely makes a positive statement towards tune-making, and this blend, certainly, makes Indian film music unique and popular, too. The composers who have the knowledge of *ragas* and chord progressions with the ability to make hybrid and matrix chord progressions often end up making better tunes.

A chart below shows the relation of *thaat* with chord progressions which can be used in the particular *thaats* of Indian classical music:

Thaat of Indian classical music	Basic chord progression can be used	Related chords
Bilawal SRGMPDN	C F G	Dm, Em, Am, Gdim/G7 F, G, C7
Kalyan SRGmPDNS	C D G	Em, bm
Khamaj SRGMPDNS SnDPMGRS	C F G B♭ F C	Am, Em, Gm, Dm, Ddim/G7
Bhairavi SrgMPdns	Cm/Fm, E♭, D♭, Fm, G	B♭m, Cm, Gm, B♭, A♭, C
Asavari SRgMPdnS	Cm, B♭, A♭	Alternative chord-E♭ Additional chord- Fm

| Kafi
SRgMPDnS	Cm, F, B♭	E♭, Gm, G, G7
Bhairav	Fm, C, D♭	E, B♭m
Marwa
SrGmDN	Am, D, A, C	D♭ (minimal use), D♭m, E, Fm
Poorvi
SrGMPdNS	C, E, D♭m, C	Em
Todi
SrgmPdNS	A♭, A♭m, D♭, A♭	B, Cm

(Indications: S- Sa, r-Komal re, R-Shuddh re, g-Komal ga, G-Shuddh ga, M- Shuddh ma, m-Tevra ma, P-Pa, d-Komal dha, D-Shuddh dha, n-Komal ni, N-Shuddh ni) All Shuddh swar are denoted with capital letters while small are denoting other deviations like komal or teevra swar. The basic note has been taken as C to describe. **S- unison, r- flat 2nd, R- perfect 2nd, g- flat 3rd, G- perfect 3rd, M- perfect 4th, m- augmented 4th, P- perfect 5th, d- flat 6th, D- perfect 6th, n- flat 7th, N- perfect 7th in Indian nomenclature of notes.**

IMPACT OF KNOWLEDGE AND EDUCATION IN TUNE MAKING

The knowledge of different segments of a curriculum is a factor which certainly influences the process of tune-making. However, this influence doesn't appear directly. Knowledge and education are two things that help a person become competent and see things in a broader way. Knowledge and education facilitate a person to see, to develop and to accept new ideas, whether it is academic or practical life issues. These two factors enable one to develop a larger vision towards the world, ethnicities, and humanity.

Apart from academics, knowledge and education can also be counted under experience. Larger experience indicates how much an individual might have learnt. It is true that better learning translates into a better experience of life. Be it from academics or other parts of life, every person learns by doing things, and achieves his experience through learning.

Both academics and life experiences affect the vision and aesthetics very strongly; it may change one's overall personality. This effect on the aesthetics of a composer affects the tune-making process, and the composer starts to imply his own experience on the tune.

AESTHETICS OF CHORDS IN TUNE MAKING

Chord itself is an element of aesthetics of music. Tunemakers or composers use the chords in many ways while making a melody, whether it is as a chord progression or the chord itself as a piece of tune. There are many ways to use chords during the conceptualisation and making of finalised structure of a tune. A composer who loves arpeggios can use arpeggiation of chords as base of tune (refer to *'Thoda Ruk Jayegi To Tera Kya Jayega'* from film *'Patanga'*). A composer who is inclined towards strumming of chords may use strumming of a chord or chords to make a good tune. This means that a composer looks at chords and perceives their usage through his aesthetic senses. The more a composer is comfortable with experimentation in chords or other musical elements, the prettier the composition will be to the world. Some composers love to use accidental chord progressions to make their tunes, while others don't. Some composers also use coloured notes with a chord.

In my case, I always go with a pattern of chords initially, and then experiment by merging different progressions. It comes out with a basic structure of melody. I don't get bothered if sometimes the pattern seems a little similar to other melodies. After getting a basic structure of a melody,

I work on making variations in the proceeding notes of the tunes. This is followed by using different motific patterns of playing styles of instruments or dynamics and other patterns of singing to get a more expressive and different melodic structure than the melody which my work resembled earlier. And finally my own melody gets a shape.

So, there are many elements of aesthetics of music which help make aesthetics towards chords in the tune-making process and which certainly gets followed by composers. These elements may be as below:

1. Amalgamation of different chord progressions
2. Coloured notes with a chord
3. Added notes
4. Chord voicing
5. Re-harmonization
6. Improvisation of chords
7. Arpeggiation of chords
8. Rhythmic patterns of chord (straddle, Alberti bass, strumming, comping etc.)
9. Augmentation, Diminution of chord
10. Different degrees of harmonies
11. Notes and scales of different style (e.g. blues and jazz).

This is a general case while making a tune on the basis of chord progressions: at the amateur level, a composer selects a key and scale, and then tries to hum or virtually play the idea or plot of tune on the instrument. If he has a mental setup of a chord progression or has recently practiced a few chords on his instrument, he would automatically be inclined towards making the composition on the basis of harmonies or chords or its extensions.

Generally, the first plot is adapted having the notes which are there in the tonic chord or scale. Later on, after having the next few notes from tonic, when the composer is satisfied or develops the instincts to work more on the composition, he selects the next chords and different progressions. During this process, the composer might shift the tonic chord from major to minor several times till he gets a desired tune. He may select different chord progressions or alternate chords or re-harmonisation process to create the feel and impression.

When composing or having a chord pattern, the composer has to be careful while using the progressions and chords. A composer selects the chords and progressions on the basis of lyrics, language, situation, twisting of words, style, and mood in the cinematic scope to make a tune. Sometimes, the beauty of melody coming from a chord progression or harmonic patterns can be made even more attractive by using accidental notes or an alien chord interrupting in between and creating an overflow of emotions.

It is not always necessary to initiate the composition from the tonic chord or scale. To attain beauty, a composer should be ready to work on any frame—be it traditional or new. There are many Indian composers, who have worked on harmonies and chords and developed a new sound, incorporated Indian notes in western melodies, and made Indian cinematic music as one of the world's most popular styles. Many times, on the basis of situation and appeal of beauty, the composer might pick up the tune, not from tonic but from supertonic; sometimes it may be dominant seventh or, perhaps, even secondary dominant. After exploring these extraordinary and accidental patterns, when one returns home i.e. tonic, the abnormality creates an altogether different atmosphere and mood. This phenomenon might work great sometimes, but it may not be acceptable all the time in the context of Indian film tunes.

Thus, we can conclude that enormous patterns of melodies can be beautified in many ways after understanding the beauty of chords and harmonies.

Effects of Aesthetics of Composer on Tune – Own Aesthetics and Borrowed Aesthetics (Inspiration)

Aesthetics is an attribute which certainly affects the tune of a composer. Moreover, aesthetics actually determines the type and uniqueness of the tune of the composer. This is the composer's own aesthetic sense to feel, to work, and to treat a tune. In accordance with the aesthetics of a composer, his tunes and styles are easily distinguishable. The aesthetics of a composer is his own peculiarity which makes an impact on the tune. It can be said that the aesthetics of a composer is actually an appearance of his stamp on tune, by which the tune may be judged.

Apart from his own aesthetics, a composer may sometimes get influenced by someone else's style of composing and adapt the peculiarities of that composer while making a tune. This might result in a tune that resembles the style of the other composer. This is called 'inspiration of style'. For example, we can discuss a song '*Ye Parbaton Ke Dayre Ye Shaam Ka Dhuan*', composed by music composer Chitragupt. The style of this song does not match with most of his other songs. From the start, this song's tune and orchestration sounds similar to Shankar-Jaikishan's songs. This was obvious and a trendy style of Shankar-Jaikishan, but Chitragupt adapted the composer duo's style for this song. You can compare the song with many of Shankar-Jaikishan's songs like "*Kaun Hai Jo Sapno Mein Aaya*" or "*Aaja Re Aa Zara, Lehra Ke Aa Zara*". In my opinion, this is an inspiration of style and texture of the composer.

One very popular song '*Kyu Aage Pichhe Dolte Ho Bhanwaron Ki Tarah*' (from the 2006 film, Golmaal) is an adaptation and blend of O. P. Nayyar's texture and style. Music composer Tushar Bhatia also adapted O. P. Naiyyar's style as a whole for the film, '*Andaz Apna Apna*'. One cannot recognise the songs in the movie as Tushar Bhatia's compositions.

Jatin-Lalit's song *"Wada Raha Sanam"* from the movie Khiladi sounds a lot like R. D. Burman's work. If you recollect some songs of R. D. Burman like *'Agar Tum Na Hote'* or *'Tune O Rangeele Kaisa Jadu Kiya'*, you will see their resemblance in terms of style with *'Wada Raha Sanam'*.

A popular track from *Khiladi 786*, *'O Balma'*, is also a track which borrowed aesthetics of R. D. Burman. This song is composed by Himesh Reshammiya, but the style of interlude for the second stanza of the R. D. Burman's song "Yamma Yamma" from the film *Shaan* is clearly followed in *'O Balma'*. The chord progression and orchestration for this song almost sounds like R. D. Burman's style in the *'Yamma Yamma'*.

These are some examples of borrowed aesthetics and it is so common in Indian film industry. If it is done carefully and correctly, borrowed aesthetics also perform very well in terms of quality and commercial success.

Sometimes, a composer does not follow the texture and style of someone else. Instead of this, he picks up a tune of another composer and then he makes his inputs of his own style and texture on that tune. It is also called inspiration for the tune. The famous song of Salil Chaudhary *'Itna Na Mujhse Tu Pyar Badha, Ki Mai Ik Badal Awara'* is an Indianised adaptation of Mozart's symphony No. 40. Shankar Jaikishan's song *'Gumnam Hai Koi'* is another such example, which was inspired by Henry Mancini's Charade.

Creativity is all about aesthetic processes towards any art form. Until you complete your own aesthetic process at a certain time for a song, your creativity is not going to get the right result. It also means that the aesthetic sense has to be further developed for the particular work. This is because aesthetics affects the tune, whether it is the composer's original or borrowed.

Chapter 4

Orchestration

"A song should never look naked in arrangement. There must be sensible filling of instruments in the background otherwise the efforts will go in vain. Look at Sebastian's work. He has made incredible statements in his songs as arranger. He has done sensible filling. Nobody had ever done this before. Listen to Kersi Lord's 'Tum Jo Mil Gaye Ho' from Hanste Zakhm. He used runs of violin groups from scale to scale. I did a song for the film 'Shahenshah' and used only major chords in the songs."

-Amar Haldipur

DEFINE ORCHESTRA AND ORCHESTRATION

The orchestration is considered one of the noblest creations of Western civilization. I agree with this comment. Orchestra basically is a group of instruments, which are played simultaneously with many partitions like melody, harmony, rhythm, etc. An orchestra includes both instruments and vocals. A composer's work is incomplete until he gets the orchestra involved in his composition. Orchestra is a physical denotation of a composer's idea to a tune. Thus the orchestra is a face rather than a body of the composer's tune. Orchestra is a means of presenting a composition. It includes a combination of instruments.

Orchestration is the planning according to which the orchestra is utilised in such a way that the beauty and the expression of a composition is able to reach its highest qualitative attributes. Through orchestration, a composer presents his thoughts musically. This is a way to have a musical dialogue between the composer and his listeners. Through orchestration, a composer distributes his musical structure into segments of different instruments. It totally depends upon the aesthetics of the composer or orchestrator.

Orchestration techniques and the art can be earned with experience and exposure, and they become the composer's personal trait after a particular point. That is why every artist has its own kind of orchestration style. Two students of the same teacher will have different styles in their work because of their own peculiarities of artistic expression.

Orchestration also involves a highly-personalised thought process of the composer or the orchestrator. Thus, the aesthetic sense is developed over the years, and gets reflected in musical works like tunemaking or orchestration. This aesthetic sense is a result of a coordination between the brain and ears. By interpreting different musical elements, this coordination enables the composer to arrive at a final decision on beauty which helps him pick colours of tones, harmonies, styles, genre and blends.

To acquire orchestration skills, one needs to have proper education and training. The process has become very sophisticated nowadays. In the Indian film music Industry, most of the music directors get their orchestration done by orchestrators, also known as arrangers. In the industry, there are so many musicians who have worked as arrangers, or even as assistants to the music composers, and eventually helped write the success stories of the composers. Some renowned music arrangers are Sebastian, Johnny Gomes, Anthony Gonsalves, Basu Chakroborthy, Uttam Singh, Manohari Singh, Jai Kumar Parte, Chic Chocolate, Chris Perry, Amar Haldipur and Kishore Sharma. These names have been known to work with music directors like Shankar-Jaikishan, O. P. Nayyar, Salil Chaudhary (Sebastian D'souza and Dattaram), R. D. Burman (Basu Chakroborthy, Manohari Singh), Madan Mohan (Master Sonik, Kersi Lord), C Ramachandra (Chic Chocolate), Chitragupt (Johnny Gomes), Rajesh Roshan (Amar Haldipur), Shiv Hari (Kishore Sharma) and Ram Laxman (Uttam Singh) etc. It was their aesthetics for orchestration with these composers which contributed to the glory of the Indian film music.

Laxmikant-Pyarelal were the only music directors who arranged their own music (done by Pyarelal). Pyarelal added a more harmonious and different sound to Indian cinema, especially in terms of harmonies and Indian rhythm's variations along with pairing, grouping and thickening of sound in rhythm instruments. Over the years, this rhythmic trend was followed by others, too.

SANGAT OR ACCOMPANIMENT VS. ORCHESTRATION (SOLOISM VERSUS GROUPISM)

Sangat, in Hindi, means 'company'. In Indian classical music, *sangat* is a well-known term for accompaniment. It is well understood in Hindustani music. *Sangat* is basically done to follow, support and enhance the main performer's presentation. So, we can say that *sangat* is thoroughly an accompaniment to support and follow the main performer. More or less, it is an unorganised accompaniment based on the artist's instant creativity and prior experience, and of course, expertise in the accompanying instrument. It basically involves soloism where the accompanist's performance comes out contingently. The same performer with the same accompanist may get varied accompaniments depending on different factors.

Since the human voice was the main voice heard in society, a long time ago, *sangat* or accompaniment was just an imitation of the human voice to support and enrich it at the time of social gatherings and festival proceedings. Ancient Greek writings indicate that in their time, instrumental music was used only to accompany dance, drama, or song or simply to imitate the human voice.[16] This was referred to as *sangat* in Indian terms, which is to support the main performer. So, *sangat* or accompaniment can be said to have been in fashion even before orchestration. We can assume that *sangat* came into existence in musical performances to enhance the performer's effect. It is believed that until about the 17th Century, instruments were relegated to the role of accompanist in western music since vocal music was the most important body of composed works.[17]

Indian classical music still uses a lot of *sangat* for practices and performances as a regard to the tradition. Orchestration

---

[16] Adler, Samuel. Study of orchestration. W.W. Norton & Company Inc., Second edition 1989, p.569.
[17] Ibid, p.569.

for pure Indian classical music is yet to come up with ease, though the Indian film music adapted orchestration, instead of *sangat*, very early in its development process. Around 1945-50, in spite of many instruments doing *sangat* to the vocalist, music directors got inclined toward using orchestration to compose songs. They started using different orchestration techniques.

The basic difference between *sangat* and orchestration is just the organisation in performance. The *sangat* is much more intended toward spontaneous creative reaction by the accompanist while orchestration involves proper planning by the composer. *Sangat* is a soloistic phenomenon while orchestration goes with a feel of groupism. Both are important in their own ways. Orchestration, in India, is basically derived from western music. Till around 1965, film songs in India were made on both *sangat* pattern and orchestration. Vocals of most songs were accompanied by basic melody on instruments. At the same time, preludes and interludes were developing in terms of harmonisation and reharmonisation. In the same time period, some music composers were inclined towards harmonious orchestration, few restricted themselves to use harmonies, and others used harmonies at a very limited level. So, there was no particular pattern followed for using harmonies. But the basic development of orchestration—from accompaniment to a group leading pattern—happened long ago in western music. Throughout the 17th Century, the orchestral task of accompaniment greatly expanded, enhanced and refined as the concerto grosso and solo concerto grew and developed.[18]

In Indian film music, orchestration became an important part in the 1950s-1960s, almost 200 years after the period of Bach and Handel came to an end around in 1750, and from where western music got new approaches toward orchestration

---

[18] Ibid, p.569.

techniques and trends with Mannheim school, Haydn and Mozart. Before 1750, composers and musicians were inclined towards stabilisation of the whole orchestra. After that, many quality developmental aspects were added to the orchestration. By the late 19th Century, the 'large orchestra' was an accepted norm. Not only the size of the orchestra increased, but also the sophistication of the use.

Initially, vocals in Indian film music were accompanied by an orchestra. This was done by having the same lead tune played on different instruments. As composer's exposure to world music grew larger, *sangat* gradually got replaced by different orchestration techniques. Those trained in western music significantly changed the way of arranging music, from simple pattern to full orchestral and chordal music.

PRINCIPAL OF ORCHESTRATION

The principles regarding the orchestration job are quite clear when it comes to writing the score. But, to develop the perception about what has to be written, it is a psycho-analytical procedure. Sometimes, it may be an obvious idea or sometimes it may be just a trial-and-error until one gets a satisfactory idea. The division of whole harmonies and all other musical elements into different segments is the basic function of orchestration. The planning of orchestration or writing a score for a song involves a broader working area.

As far as planning for the orchestration to make a song is concerned, it involves rough design of orchestral arrangements, like the intro music, thematic phrases, backing instrumental and vocals, counterpoints, climax point, modulations, solos, ensemble passes, re-harmonisation of basic melodic structure, rhythms, etc. At any moment, the composer can change his previously-planned music for a better idea. For planning the orchestration, you can refer to the previous chapter where we have discussed the thought process of making a tune.

The principles of orchestration are just the technical aspects to write different segments of instruments. Orchestration requires one to take a given arrangement and assign it in parts to different instruments, usually in the form of a written score. Before writing, it is important to have detailed knowledge of the concerned instrument regarding timbre, pitch, dynamics, playing techniques, and limitations. Some instruments do not sound in the basic key of composition and these should be written by transposition of notation so that instrument can be used in the best way.

Mismatching tones should strictly be rectified before the performance of any orchestra. Crystal clear writing of a score is a must in terms of selection of instruments, pitches, tones, dynamics and harmonies to be presented. The number of instruments and total size of the orchestra has to be decided well before the start of the score-writing.

Apart from knowing about the instruments, a composer should also be well-versed with the techniques of writing and, of course, the type of media for which the orchestration is being done. The basic principle of orchestration is writing music for different instrumental combinations according to their timbre, playing technique and aesthetic value in the composition for which the orchestration is being done.

Better knowledge about the peculiarities of instruments, different musical elements and richer experiences leads to a good orchestration. Rimsky-Korsakov and Walter Piston had given a huge illustration regarding different segments and instruments in reference to orchestration, which is still considered among the pioneer works in the area of orchestration.

The discussions made by Alan Belkin are helpful if one wants to have a better understanding of orchestration. His thoughts about good orchestration can be treated as the basic principles of orchestration, especially in the light of aesthetics. For a good orchestration, he argues for clarity and audibility of each instrument and their phrases or parts, change of orchestration at the right place and with appropriate degree of contrast, supply of sufficient variety and freshness of colours of musical elements, fair chances for players to put their individual feel in playing, and creating overall richness through use of multiple planes of tones.

As far as Indian music is concerned, the orchestration of a song is planned on the basis of visuals planned to be shot for the particular scene of the movie. Many composers go for the obvious and trending ideas of orchestration in reference to location, situation, mood, emotion etc. though experimentations are also done from time to time.

For film music, some traits and trends guide the composer to work on the orchestration for a particular song. For example, if a girl is heartbroken after a break-up scene, then there will be deep, sad instrumental on sarangi or violin with *aalapkari* for the background score, which may be followed by a sad song. In contrast, if a scene is about the blooming relationship between a boy and a girl with a lot of fascination and romance, then there will be a fast jhala on sitar or santoor, or a fast running string orchestra covered up with huge chorus or maybe a pleasant strumming of guitar. These kinds of elements are trendy in film songs and background music. Sitar, santoor, guitar and mandolin alongwith strings are mostly used in romantic situations. For example, watch the song '*Jaagi Hui Fizayen*' from the film '*Aur Pyar Ho Gaya*'. You will hear a heavy runs of string section followed by mandolin and flute, which definitely travels in the scene accurately. After the entry of electronic music, the scenario has changed because acoustic instruments have been replaced in majority and there is a huge range of electronic and virtual instruments, but mostly without proper character. So, the trends are a little bit suspended in music for a few years, otherwise the audience's nerves are well connected with the trends discussed here.

As a whole, the principles of orchestration are administered by aesthetics and the needs of the composer. Orchestration for Indian film music songs is mostly ruled by the trends settled in the last six to seven decades. Though the newly-arrived electronic music goes a little beyond the old trends, these synthetic sounds and procedures don't make a true aesthetic vision towards orchestration. This is an issue which needs to be resolved soon for the sake of better music in Indian films. Having said so, there are still some areas in electronic music which have scope or have hit the right marks in terms of vision and aesthetics.

SECTIONS OF MUSICAL INSTRUMENTS AND VOCALS

According to western music literature, there are four major categories of instruments:

- Ensemble
- Brass
- Woodwind
- Percussion instruments and keyboard

Each category has further sub-categorised, but we will discuss the four major categories.

THE ENSEMBLE

This is the section of the violin group. It contains violins, violas, violoncellos (cello) and double basses. There may be viola d'Amore, too. The ratio of these instruments may be as follows:

16 first violins, 14 second violins, 12 violas, 10 cellos and 8 basses i.e. 16, 14, 12, 10, 8.

The number of instruments may vary as per requirement, like 12, 10, 8, 6, 4 or 8, 6, 4, 3, 2 respectively. Standard ensemble for studios may be of 6, 6, 4, 4. The string section is known for its versatility and the instruments have an equality of tone throughout the range.

In the string section, extreme changes of dynamics can be used effectively in a very short span of time. This is the most capable section for emotional expressions. A very pleasant texture of strings can be used for a prolonged period without making the listener tired. Irrespective of the range of the instrument, there are specific characteristics. In his book, *Principles of Orchestration*, Rimsky-Korsakov describes the top string of each instrument as follows: violin – brilliant, viola – biting and nasal, cello – chest voice, and double bass – penetrating.

The string sub-category has a high acceptability in orchestration due to variety, sound and ability to be used indifferent tonal planes simultaneously. In Indian film industry, strings came very early in use, but the importance of this section was first shown and propagated by Shankar-Jaikishan (with their assistant Sebastian D'Souza and team), and later followed and developed by other composers.

For strings, there are specific and different bowing patterns such as Legato, Staccato, Spiccato, Detache, Loure, Marcaeto, Jete, Tremolo, Col Legno, Ponticello, Sul Tasto, Flautando, Glissando/Portamento, Sul G etc. Alan Belkin emphasised on another peculiarity of string section as pizzicato i.e., percussive sound produced by this segment.[19] The timbre quality of this pizzicato is unique, and somehow, it is one of the best choices when it is used as percussive phrases. This can not be compared to another percussion sound.

The string sub-category is the richest in overtones, and most powerful and versatile section in orchestration as it has a broad spectrum of timbre, playing techniques, and dynamics. In Indian film music, as it achieved the developed orchestration

---

[19] Belkin, Alan. Artistic Orchestration. 2001, p.6. www.dolmetsch.com/O.pdf.

patterns with the influence of western music, the string section became key in soundtracks. This is a unanimously-accepted and used segment of orchestration all over the world. This is possibly because strings can be easily blended with almost any style of music.

About the peculiarities of the strings section, Walter Piston wrote, "They have a greater dynamic range than wind instruments and far more expressive capacity. The tone colour of the string group is fairly homogenous from top to bottom, variations in the different registers being much more subtle than in the winds."[20] The string section has no barriers. That's why, any kind of mood, emotion, musical patterns, style and character can be assigned to perform in this section without any hesitation. It is known to always deliver in full capacity. Its versatility gives it greater and broader acceptability, and musicians are aware about this level of acceptance.

If we see the orchestration of Indian film songs, string instruments gained prominence in the early years itself. In my opinion, the string section is the backbone of orchestration for any kind of music. In areas where strings are not used because of tradition (eg. folk music in India and across the world), its addition will certainly enrich the charm and beauty of that music.

Brass

Brass instruments are usually played by the performer's mouth. Keeping the lips on a cup-shaped mouthpiece, the performer forces air stream into the instrument which produces a tone. The pipes and mouthpieces come in different types and shapes. These instruments generate great power in music with subtlety and versatility. Some of the basic brass instruments are horns, trumpet, trombone, tuba, clarinet, and euphorium.

---

[20] Piston, Walter. Orchestration. Victor Gollancz Ltd. London, 1969, p.3.

The average brass section consists of 4 horns, 3 trumpets, 3 trombones and one tuba. However, this may vary depending upon the need of composition and aesthetics of the composer.

Many musicians think that brass instruments have not been used as much as instruments from other categories, in orchestrations. It may be so because of the structure or the lack of expressiveness in the playing techniques. Each brass instrument has its limitations related to its construct or playing. For instance, I have heard that double tonguing is tough in big mouthpiece instruments. The use of stopped notes and mutes alters the character of brass tone. Hence, they are mostly employed on trumpets, cornets and horns.

Breathing techniques for brass instruments are very much similar to the woodwind section. A great similarity of tones and timbre is present in the instruments of this category. Brass instruments can be used for melodic, rhythmic, contrapuntal, and harmonic roles in playing. In ancient times, brasses were used for doubling the human voices. Till the early 19th century, brass instruments were not as developed as they are today; they were not equipped with pistons, valves etc. At that time, they were played on the principle of over blowing to get the harmonic series as desired. A longer tube was used to lower pitch production. Samuel Adler believes that the skill of an individual brass player is determined by "his ability to find any notated pitch (or partial) by a combination of embouchure and breath control."[21]

Brass instruments require a great amount of breathing technique while being played. Composers must take this factor into account while composing for these instruments. The piece should be written as per the required breathing patterns. If a slur phrase has to be performed, it should be written for a

---

[21] Adler, Samuel. Study of Orchestration. W.W. Norton and Company. 1989, p. 268.

single breath. These instruments have a great dynamic power and cannot be played as soft as strings or woodwinds can be.

A proper balance has to be maintained, otherwise its dynamics may adversely affect the performance of the string and woodwind instruments. Mutes are used in the playing of brass instruments and it gives a feeling of softness. There are different types of mutes, like straight mute, cup mute, Harmon or wa-wa mute, whispa mute, solo tone, etc. There are also various types of attacks like sforzando and forte piano attack, light soft fast tonguing, double tonguing, triple tonguing, and flutter tonguing. Glissandi—produced by lip slur in brass segment— is most effective in the upper register. Trills and tremolos are another major character of this category, however it is complicated. Tremolos have a smaller success ratio than trills as trills are very much executable on brass instruments. To enhance smooth playing, some crooks and slides are also installed in the brass category to work according to the written orchestration.

Woodwind

As the name suggests, this category comprises wooden instruments such as flute, clarinet etc., although, in the modern age, they are made of metal also. It is a group of all heterogeneous instruments. The balance can be made by master players of these different types of instruments in terms of dynamics, timbre, blend etc. Samuel Adler suggested classifying woodwind instruments in five ways i.e., by families, by the kind of reed used, by the shape of pipe, by whether they transpose or not, etc.[22] Further, he divided instruments by families as flute family (Piccolo, flute, etc.), oboe family (oboe, English horn, bassoon, etc), clarinet family (clarinet basset horn) and saxophone family (sopranino, alto, tenor, baritone, etc). In terms of classification based on reed, there

---

[22] Ibid, p.153.

are non-reed woodwinds (all flutes), single reeds (all clarinet and saxophone), and double reed (oboe, bassoon etc). On the basis of the shape of the pipe, there are cylindrical tubes, a straight pipe (flute, clarinet), and conical tube (oboe, bassoon and saxophone). In the classification based on 'over blow', there are conical pipe woodwinds, flute, and clarinet. Based on the transposition, the classifications are: non-transposing woodwinds (flute, oboe and bassoon), and transposing woodwinds (Piccolo, Alto Flute, English Horn, Clarinet etc)

Vibrato is a general characteristic of woodwind instruments as it is found in ensembles. Composers should write the indication for engaging vibrato or non-vibrato, for interesting effects as per the need of the orchestration. Articulations are done by tonguing in the woodwind section. Flutter tongue is another special effect, produced by fast rolling of the tongue. Alan Belkin wrote about how woodwinds can provide "intimate solo effects" due to their various distinctive timbres.[23] The effects are the basic affectivity of these instruments in orchestration. This soloistic nature allows the instruments to work out for a wide range of expression and emotion. Without understanding the dynamics and tonal registers of each instrument, a composer cannot utilise this section effectively. Close intervals in harmony help with the blend. Since most woodwinds have rich overtones, musicians don't go for wider intervals. This nature of woodwinds is also a reason why they are generally used in pairs, threes or fours for harmonic addition as well as the thickness of sound.

Apart from expression, woodwind instruments are good at adding colours to the different harmonic parts of composition. Nicolas Rimsky-Korsakov defined the 'scope of greatest expression' in the woodwind section as "the range in which the instrument is best qualified to achieve the various grades of tone. (forte, piano, cresc., dim, sforzando,

---

[23] Belkin, Alan. Artistic Orchestration. 2001, p.6. www.dolmetsch.com/O.pdf.

morendo etc.)—the register which admits of the most expressive playing, in the truest sense of the word."[24] His argument is that when a wind instrument goes beyond this range, it becomes more prominent and useful to enrich the colour of music or note. Rimsky-Korsakov believed that outside this range, the wind is more notable for richness of colour than for the expression.

PERCUSSION INSTRUMENTS AND KEYBOARD

I believe that percussion instruments are the most ancient as they have known to be a part of folk music. There almost seems to be an innumerable variety of these instruments in both pitched and non-pitched categories. We will talk about the percussion instruments which are normally used in orchestration. Apart from being categorised into pitched and non-pitched, percussion instruments can also be classified scientifically into membranophones (with a vibrating membrane stuck with an object such as various drums), and others which are made up of wood, metal or different material (which can produce sound, such as triangles, cymbal bells, rings, khadtal etc.). Another classification of this segment is: the standard percussion section, auxiliary percussion instruments, sound effects and exotic instruments.[25]

The standard section includes kettle drums, snare drums, cymbals, triangles, tambourine, glockenspiel etc. Auxiliary percussion instruments are instruments used as substitutes for standard groups (like castanets, xylophone, tenor drum, vibraphones etc). Sound effects are the sounds used for extra effects by imitation or real sounds by wood blocks, water drops, sand papers etc. Exotic instruments are normally Latin-origin instruments, but can be of any tribal origin.

---

[24] Rimsky-Korsakov, Nicolas. Principles of Orchestration. E.F. Kalmus Orchestra Scores Incorporated, p.14.
[25] Piston, Walter. Orchestration. Victor Gollancz Ltd. London, 1969, pp.296-297.

Due to inclusion of both pitched and non-pitched instruments in this category, percussion instruments can be used for rhythm as well as for melody, resonance and transitional sounds, totally depending upon the usage according to the aesthetics of the composer. Many pitched instruments may also be used as percussion instruments (like piano, guitar, cello etc).

KEYBOARD INSTRUMENTS

All the instruments with keyboard fall under this category, including piano, celesta, harpsichord, harmonium, accordion, ondes martenot, and organ. Conventionally, piano was the instrument to guide the rhythm and give the pitched and melodic colour to the rhythm segment and, of course, to support the weak places. Its role was substantially similar to that of harpsichord. Later, piano got used as a solo instrument for concertos by using all orchestras in accompaniment, like in many compositions of Mozart and Beethoven. Arpeggios, tremolos, repeated block chords, sustained chords, stride style, boogie etc. are some of the most used characters in this category. Harmonium is an instrument with small reeds.

Maurice Martenot invented ondes Martenot in 1928. In this electrical instrument, the tones are produced in pulsation by two different frequency currents. Normally, keyboard instruments have register in all pitches and octaves available on the keyboard.

VOCALS

Composing for vocals is a tough part of orchestration because human voices have a small range and register. Writing for voices seeks careful considerations about register and timbre quality. It also may vary from one to another singer. Very low and high notes may be problematic for some singers. Hence, the composer should consider the common discomfort level when writing for vocals. When it comes to bands, in accompanying the voice, the orchestral score should be written very soothingly and light so that the singer can give all the different shades of expression without any variation in the tonal quality of voice. In moments where full voice is required, the singer should be provided nice support by the orchestra. Expression and hardness of the tones may sometimes contradict each other. So, the composer should check how comfortable the singer is with singing different scales. For writing the vocals, the orchestral part also needs to be considered for effectiveness.

WRITING FOR DIFFERENT SEGMENTS FOR A TUNE'S EXPRESSION

Expressing is the utmost goal of any music. Writing for different categories of instrument for any tune or melody seeks highest priority towards its expressiveness for the audience and of course for the media it is to be created. Although these performative means of expression are very technical in use, they still have the power to reveal the beauty of the tune. Some of these technical aspects are articulations, dynamics, cadences, progressions, accents, passage plans and textures of sounds, fade in and outs etc.

The different ways of expressing through musical elements are "dynamics, tempo, emphasis of beats, and articulation. Tuning has to be considered especially for the interpretation of several ethnic music in proper style. Effects can be classified into two categories, technical and articulation effects."[26] Dynamics is all about the loudness of sound, while articulation tells us how a note is treated in the timeline or how it gets divided within a timepiece through the playing technique's peculiarities.

---

[26] Berndt, Axel; Theisel, Holger. Adaptive Musical Expression from Automatic Real Time Orchestration and Performances. http://wwwpub.zih.tu-dresden.de/~aberndt/publications/ICIDS08-2.pdf

A composer goes through many such technical aspects to arrive at a particular mood and expression of tune. In this regard, a discussion has also been made earlier under the topic '*Thought process of making a tune*' in the previous chapter. Alan Belkin has discussed many factors which can work for artistic orchestration for better effectiveness in terms of expression. The factors described by him are: accents, cadences, progressions, gradually rising or falling passages, texture getting thicker or thinner, gradation of climaxes, overlapping and fadeouts, change of sound, rate of orchestral change, degree of continuity/contrast, registers, colour, sustained versus dry sounds, fat versus thin sound, unison doubling, balance—simultaneous and successive, etc. A composer must consider these factors while doing orchestration.

Aesthetics of chords in Making Orchestra Of A Tune

The aesthetics of chords is all about the selection process of certain chords in a certain place of composition so that the utmost expression of a musical thought can be obtained through the chord and its division into various instruments to get the perfect sound according to the need of beauty. In this regard, Walter Piston wrote, "Each chord ought to be seen in its setting in the score."[27] The usage of chord is a totally subjective matter when making a tune or orchestration. If we talk about orchestration of an already-existing melody, some chords are very obvious while some chords are perceived through the aesthetic sense of the composer; aesthetics come into play when chord progressions are made for a tune.

Indian film songs are mostly divided in parts like prelude, *mukhada* (main title lines of lyrics), interlude, *antara* (stanza) and ending. Some might also have an unplugged part or a rhythmic prelude. Prelude provides a hook or pickup to the *mukhda*. *Mukhda* is the face of a song which comes

---
[27] Piston, Walter. Orchestration. Victor Gollancz Ltd., 1969, p.396.

repeatedly in the whole song, usually after each *antara*. Apart from the obvious chords that will come in the orchestration, there may be many alternative chords in some points of the orchestration—including where the basic melody has to be rendered. The composer should have the ability to analyse the aesthetics to decide which chord should be finalised for every spot in his composition. This decision can not be made by any rule. What has been used previously by other people may only be helpful in this regard.

Reaching on finalisation of chords, the implementation of selected chords is done through division in different segments of instruments. When this division is done, the balance of registers, tonality, spacing, blend of tone colours, tutti chords, dynamic levels, range and pitch location are the factors which has to be taken into account so that maximised effect of chords can be obtained in terms of expression of the tune.

A balanced chord produces a flat vertical plane of sound where single voices are not prominent but the whole effect comes out by a natural sound of consonance and dissonance. This balance of sonority is achieved because of a healthy interaction between the composer and the player, and of course, the composer's experience level. Wherever a composer finds a weak register of an instrument, he can go for unison doubling for that particular portion.

Tonality is a very important factor, when harmonies come through progressions. Sometimes, there are reasons for having some tones stronger than others for a chord. "One of these concerns is the tonal function of the chord. Being structurally more important to the tonality, the tonal degrees of the key (tonic, dominant and sub-dominant) may be doubled more than the modal degrees (mediant and sub-mediant)."[28] But this should be employed in the light of beauty. Spacings made for

---

[28] Piston, Walter. Orchestration. Victor Gollancz Ltd., 1969, p.447.

chords and passing of overtones should be made very clear so that harmonic structure doesn't get deviated. The ideal spacing usually comes in the root positioned major chord.

Colouring the notes of a chord in different registers is an efficient way to get better expressions of mood. Tutti chords are normally used in the climax point of a tune or in the endings. Thick sound instruments, like brass and high pitched woodwind instruments, are used to get the desired tutti chord implementation. For a good orchestration, create a basic plan of the chord at start, and then move for further details in the written score. Conclusively, there should be a plan, on the basis of which the score can be written correctly with terms of techniques and beauty.

There are technical aspects which help with the expression of tune through orchestration. These may be treated as the ruling factors, but not as rules because expression is the most important issue for an end user i.e. listener of the tune, and anything can be overruled for the sake of the listener. The composer works on the orchestration of a tune according to his aesthetics and he judges the beauty from the point of a listener, especially in Indian film music.

Chapter 5

Aesthetics of Composer in Perceptual Process of a Tune

"It's important to learn first what one does not need to do. Any chord can be good but is it useful for song? It is important to know the limitations of any implementation. An appropriate quantity of sugar makes the tea tasty, neither less nor more. A fixed quantity of the ingredients is the decisive factor of beauty of the result."

-Amar Haldipur

CULTURAL, SOCIAL, ECONOMIC BACKGROUND AND LEARNING OF COMPOSER

As a composer, I have always valued learning in my life. It is only through the continuous process of learning that a composer ultimately develops his aesthetics. Some of the factors that affect this process are the cultural, social, economical, and educational backgrounds of an individual.

It can be said that every facet of a person's life contributes to their learning. The process begins right at birth, and the cultural, social, economical, and educational factors trickle in over time to shape the individual's knowledge and understanding. The richer the socio-cultural values, the richer is the experience level of the composer, thereby upscaling his individual creativity.

Liveliness, which is the feeling of being 'alive', helps nurture sensitivity in any composer or an artist; creativity never comes in isolation. It is liveliness that sparks sensitivity inside a creative individual and further fuels it. As sensitivity increases, the thirst to venture into newer dimensions grows stronger. This thirst turns into an urge to create something, thereby unleashing the highest levels of creativity.

Our brain uses experiences as raw materials to get pleasure. Every individual has their own unique way of deriving pleasure because of different experiences and responses to various aspects of life. Experience and sensitivity result in pleasure. This sensitivity induces experience to create pleasure from the different aspects of life. It is important to know that our sensitivity originates from our concerns, affections, and trust. Our peculiar individuality comes into existence because of sensitivity. Our vision is the measure of our sensitivity. As we feel concerned, we get closer to perception of integrity, intimacy and liveliness. This perception develops the love and further gets converted into trust. Only after forming this trust, we perceive sense. This sense is an indication of our sensitivity.

Sensitivity is the causing factor of a composer's aesthetic perception. When we become capable of fulfilling the visible and invisible thirst of the audience because of his sensitivity, the result is nothing less than beautiful. This deep understanding increases our aesthetic sense, through which we acquire our creative individuality. Every human has his/her own level of sensitivity, which also means the aesthetic sense differs from person to person. The individuality of a person makes his creativity different from others. By acquiring this distinctive characteristic, a person enters an indefinite circle of creativity. This peculiarity leaves him with two choices, either to follow the traditional ways or experiment.

In the social aspect, there are so many factors that contribute to the aesthetic senses. When people are motivated by duties to the 'collectives', which they construe themselves as a part of, it is called collectivism. On the other hand, individualism is a pattern in which individuals see themselves as independent of collectives. Individualists prefer unusual things while collectivists prefer common things in life. The feelings of 'similarity' and 'commonness' in the collectivists affects their cognitive style. The same thing happens with individualists, whose cognitive and aesthetic senses are affected by their feeling of uniqueness.

This is all linked to the thought process of creative people, which is said to be holistic. All the backgrounds of learning, whether it is social, cultural, educational or whatever, are the constituents of the learning process of a composer or any artist.

The background and upbringing of a composer certainly makes a difference to his learning and his creations. If I have spent my growing years in Baghelkhand-Bundelkhand region of Madhya Pradesh, the culture I was surrounded by will find its way in my compositions. Similarly, if I have grown up in India, the diverse cultures will affect my creations. In a generalized way, a listener who follows music across different ethnicities and countries can easily differentiate between Italian music and a Latin composition. The musical traits and trends of the culture, and the society to which the composer belongs or has a personal connection, become associated with his thoughts and perceptions. R.D. Burman often used Latin beats in his songs just because he loved it and got his thoughts associated with that kind of music. It became a part of R.D. Burman's aesthetic sense. In classical Indian music, the usual base of music and compositions is the raga system. So, most Indian composers also end up improvising on that framework.

I feel that the cultural background is the main point from where the natural process of development of aesthetics begins. This is because, in my opinion, culture includes the trends and traditions of the surroundings of the person. The cultural traits are easily accessible to the person at any time and the only thing that matters is how well he relates to the traits and how they affect his choices.

The social background is similar to the cultural background when it comes to the learning process of a composer. A "good" society gives good traits and a "bad" society gives bad ones. A good accompaniment facilitates all surroundings to be wise and honest. A man is known by his company which he keeps, and this company will have some effect on his aesthetic sense.

Our gurus and teachers always push us to have good social surroundings in order to make us wise beings. This wisdom of a person makes him a good artist, whether he composes or writes or pursues any other form of art. The essential thing is that a person must have a good social, cultural, educational background so that he may follow a wise approach with a sense of social and moral responsibility while making his creations.

Good education, irrespective of the stream, helps a person inculcate the necessary traits and skills. These traits are adaptability, acceptability, openness, proactiveness, competence, confrontation etc., which positively contribute to the creative process.

We have already discussed how education and knowledge in tune making affect the creative process and learning of a composer. The linkage of cultural, social, educational background to the aesthetics, or rather the learning process, of the composer gives him the skills of balance, harmony, unity, and order. These basic skills always play a role in the creative thinking and thought process of an artist.

Knowledge and education, along with social and cultural backgrounds, contribute to perception and aesthetics of a composer. His understanding of different elements of this world like nature, geography, psychology, ecology, history etc. contributes to the result of his artistic creations.

As far as the composition for Indian film music is concerned, one needs to have a broader knowledge and experience of life. The cinematic music of India always has a 'larger than life' appeal to it. So, it necessarily requires greater life experience and experimental creative process to fulfill the needs of a larger-than-life cinematic act. Except for the background score— which is composed on the visuals — the songs made for films are pre-recorded, and then the visuals are shot on the same. In this sense, the composer bears greater responsibility as he has to think according to the shots and scenes, which are going to be directed on his composition.

Whether or not the production process will be smoother depends on a composer's experience of cinema as well as his own experience of life. The variety of factors which affects the learning process of a composer, whether they are social, cultural, educational or sound physics-related or others, will be discussed later.

The economic background of a composer also affects his learning, though I feel that the enthusiasm of a curious mind can make any person overcome his issues. A firm and healthy economic status may facilitate a composer in many ways. He can get exposure to many records, performances and an expensive education easily because of his sound economic background. But, if a person who does not have the monetary means to have a career in music may find such opportunities out of reach, which may obstruct his learning process. Many aspiring musicians and composers fail to make it in the industry because of their poor economic background. There are very few cases in which people overcome their financial woes and make a successful career in music.

Sound Physics Factors

The factors of sound physics certainly play an important role in the aesthetics of a composer. How he thinks about a particular sound or pattern of sound depends on his learning and experience. The choice of sounds, instruments and timbres affects the design of composition and sound design of a composer. If the note C is played on piano and the singer sings the same C, a person would still be able to differentiate between the two even though they have the same pitch. This is because both the modes sound differently. All musical instruments or voices possess their own peculiar patterns of overtones, due to which each instrument has a different and unique sound texture which we call as tone color or timbre.

The timbre of instruments or human voices is the factor which affects the outcome of a composer. Simply, if a composer loves or hates some specific timbre, it will get reflected in his compositions and orchestration. If I love the violin's timbre on the higher registers, I will often use violins in higher registers than its middle or lower registers. It will reflect my aesthetics and will be seen in my compositions. In the same way, if I dislike the sound of a trumpet, then iI won't use it often in my compositions. Timbre, or more precisely, likes and dislikes to any kind of sound, plays an important role in the reflection of aesthetics of a composer. The same thing happens with the musical styles. If a composer loves a certain music style, like waltz or blues, it will also be reflected in the composer's work and aesthetics in the normal circumstances, until he is working with his own aesthetics. When it comes to borrowed aesthetics to compose, a composer simply goes with the choices of the person from whom he is borrowing the aesthetics.

If we think about solid sounds, floating sounds, sustain and release of sound, we'll find they also have a role in making the aesthetics of a composer. It is often said that the orchestra has no sustaining pedal. Alan Belkin believed that this points to an important issue in general: resonance. "Resonance is by definition a part of the background layer. In its literal meaning, it refers to echo, the effect of a 'live' room. However, orchestral, resonance can be deliberately composed and therefore individualized," wrote Belkin.[29]

Resonance certainly affects the aesthetics of the composer in terms of his choice and usage in his work. Long-held notes are sustained notes which enrich the texture of sound. They often used to highlight some important phrases. This particular way of 'composing' with resonance gives way to more refined ways of using sustained sound in the background to enrich the texture.

How does a composer use the sustained sounds? Does he like these kinds of sounds and textures? Does he use it

---

[29] Belkin, Alan. Artistic Orchestration. p.16. www.dolmetsch.com/O.pdf,

for the purpose of ornamentation or something else? Sound and textures are the variables which affect the aesthetics of a composer.

Dry sounds are normally meant for those portions in a composition with only rhythmic percussions, while wet sounds are atmospheric percussions. This dry/wet distinction is analogous to the need for a variety of articulation (staccato/legato) from a rhythmic and motific point of view. Due to human nature, a sound always develops a like or dislike in an ear. It is a biological response associated with aesthetics. Sound produces a striking reaction in our nervous system which ultimately results in the like or dislike.

Fat and thin sounds—which are ways to describe the timbre—also need to be discussed here. At the same level of dynamics, a trumpet will sound 'fat' in comparison to stringed instruments. Fat and thin distinctions of sounds are based on loudness and volume. In an orchestra, thick or fat sounds are of two ways: as chosen timbres (e.g. the French horn), or the tuba, and as a result of unison doubling. As a rule, doubling at the unison adds more volume (thickness) than force, says Belkin.

When the unison doubling is done on the same instrument, it results in quantitative improvement of sound. However, when two or more instruments are used for unison doubling, it results in both quantitative and qualitative improvement. Two or more instruments involved in unison doubling create a new color of timbre, which also changes the quality of sound. Solid sounds are fat sounds which are comparatively lesser ambient. Floating sounds are sounds with effects of slur (i.e. meend in Indian classical music), and also large ambience with flanging voices.

Sustaining notes and their releasing points adds a certain beauty to the composition if used correctly. The choices of a composer regarding these factors directly affect his aesthetic presentation and defines his level of creativity. For example, several tracks of R. D. Burman shows his inclination towards sounds of marcus, drum clapper and bass guitar which contributes to his peculiarity. Similarly, A. R. Rahman often uses synth pads for the background of his songs. These are not the only peculiarities of these composers; there are many other things that define their style and aesthetics.

The register (height of a note) of the instruments is quite definitive in terms of its type, make and category. Normal registers of instruments are obviously used. Register planning is essential for a good orchestration, because a change of register may be obvious even to a non-musician.

The occasional use of high and low registers may give contrast to a phrase. Also, sometimes, extreme registers may largely affect a certain part especially in the finishing lines. The choice of registers also affects the composition and orchestration of a composer.

Dynamics is a very important factor of sound which certainly contributes positively to aesthetics of an orchestration, if used properly. Mixing and mastering engineers are the ones who put the right dynamics to different tracks of instruments after dubbing or music programming. The usual dynamics of instruments is obvious according to their timbre and registers though better evaluation at the time when an instrument is being played and later at the time of balancing and mixing, can result in a better result in terms of dynamics. Belkin argues- The best rule for a beginner is: orchestrate your dynamics. Especially at dynamic extremes, beginners must ensure that the instruments and the registers chosen are conducive to the dynamic level required.

All the factors related to sound physics are useful in the orchestration technique and are, hence, taught in the theories and practices. However, the experience of musicians and composers is always a key factor which comes according to choices of their own. But for sure, these factors must be taken into account when music is being created.

An experienced music composer keeps all these factors in his mind when he starts his thought process of making a tune. Perception always comes from senses and experiences.

PSYCHOLOGICAL FACTORS

Making a composition or any creative work depends on many psychological factors. Any creative process includes a psychoanalytical process; imagination is the base for any artistic outcome. I feel imagination is the basic psychological factor for the composition of music. Invisible becomes visible because of the imagination.

Visualising any image, either seen before or just in thoughts, is imagination. We can say that imagination is the power that enables creation. Imagination can be defined as conceiving an invention on behalf of a perception in a lively way.

A perception followed by conceiving a musical structure is a musical imagination. Hence, this imagination is the basic psychological factor affecting the aesthetics of a music composer. Famous philosopher Sartre divided imagination into four categories i.e. image, portrait, sign and symbol. He argued that imagination and sense, both are interrelated. Imagination or sense, both cannot work in isolation for a creative process. According to this relationship of imagination and sense, imagination is divided into visual imagination, sound imagination, touch imagination, odder or smell imagination, act imagination and sentient (*ras*) imagination.

These imaginations can further be divided on personal interest. I interviewed renowned architect and engineering expert Rajendra Sharma in 2014 who told me that his imagination for a building or colony comes in the type of variants like size, mass, blocking, shadow etc. He further said that all these elements automatically come to his imagination with factors of coherence, correlation, logic and interrelation.

Everyone who is in a creative process involves their thought process led by their own psychological approach and factors. However, at a broader level, these factors belong to the same ground. Imagination adapts the procedure of extension, diminution, substitution, combination and distribution of a perception or thought.

Dr. Kumar Vimal propagated the elements of aesthetics in his own way. His interpretation is very interesting. He argued that preparation, incubation, illumination and frequency or repetitions are the four states of imagination. According to him, the traits of an imaginative person may be as follows:

More supervision ability, can view and put a particular part of a thing or hypothesis in a violent way, gets immense pleasure to see and present the unseen, culturally has more devotion, and specific power to hold on many thoughts simultaneously and can come with a broader comprehensive thought.[30]

These traits broadly describe a creative personality which have the power to imagine. So, imagination ends with the production of a virtual image. This virtual image further gets developed by more creative ideas and particular techniques of the art form. In music, the image comes in the form of time image, specific tones and intervals with the sense of feelings and emotions in the form of dynamics and other related dimensions. As far as music is concerned, the virtue of creativity is the time image of sounds which always have a different tonal quality. This tonal quality comprises

---

[30] Vimal, Kumar. Saundarya Shastra Ke Tattva. Rajkamal Prakashan, New Delhi, 5th edition, 1989, p.135.

musical notes, timbre, tempo, dynamics and all other musical specialities of sound related to music.

Some external factors in tunemaking which depend on the psychological status of composer are:

- Level of will-power, or mental toughness.
- Level of positivity of attitude.
- Level of capacity of experimentation.
- Level of flexibility of mood i.e. transition of mood so that composer may reach the right mood needed for a tune.
- Capacity of controlled and planned imagination for a particular mood or situation, correlation of senses, experience and interpretation of these in a smarter way.
- Capacity to make correlation of mood, situation with tones and intervals.
- Capacity to assess the perception and thought of a tune with all heard and composed tunes to avoid reoccurrence factor.
- Observation/supervision/survey capability- stronger level of these skills leads to more consolidated unique musical thought.
- Faster recollection of data from memory, conscious and subconscious mind.
- Super talent of assessment and self-assessment.

Emotions are also factors of psychology, found in all cultures across the globe. Emotions are responses evolved in the process of coping with challenges which leads to a great impact on life. These are the ingredients of human nature though these can be constructed by social learning and events, too. Cultural and social ethics also have a great impact on the emotional status and expression. Behavioural responses are the results of emotional expression.

Some studies suggest that performance and its relation with arousal have an inverted-U relationship. The tip of the inverted "U" is a point where the performance reaches at its highest level.

The link between symmetry and beauty has an influence on aesthetic preferences. Symmetry is always associated with beauty. Structures which are symmetrical in nature are liked more. Symmetry plays an important role in aesthetic judgment. This aesthetic judgment is nothing but the feel of beauty. The brain suggests a biological base to any structure to process the choice on which the aesthetic judgment gets carried out. This procedure also shows inverted U-shape results. Symmetry is mostly preferred as beauty perhaps because it is easier to process than complex structures. Higher perceptual fluency comes when symmetrical work is carried out. This is what I've learnt after studying various research works conducted across the globe.

Compositional balance also contributes to the aesthetic judgments. Balance gives stability to any composition by the elements like size, shape, color, arrangements and order. Many psychologists have revealed in their studies that a level of expertise in any art form gives a decision-making sense regarding the artistic perception and analysis. Expertise also tends to challenge experiences, while naiveness tends to seek pleasure. These are the factors of preference. Assumptions are also psycho-social factors i.e. tendency to see things according to image of reality.

ETHNICITY, SOCIAL & ECONOMIC FACTORS

Actually, all the economic, social, ethnicity factors are associated with the making and development of the aesthetics of a composer. These are invisible but have a great impression on the creative structures. The famous modern composer Yanni had said in a discussion that what is foreign music for him could be country music for someone else. The western part of the world labels Indian music under 'eastern music'. It is our ethnicity which gets associated with the music. Social factors have already been discussed under the topic earlier in this book.

Ethnicity, social, and economic background together contribute towards the development of aesthetic taste and sense. Ethnicity itself indicates the profile based on variation in color, language, caste etc. These variants basically develop the tastes and likes of a person since the birth. My aesthetics is what I saw, felt, and analysed for adaptations, likes, and dislikes. I prefer Indian music because I got to hear, feel, and analyse it and made a decision to like it. The same thing happens with a person who lives in Italy and thus develops a liking for Italian music. I may hesitate to hear and accept Italian music or other unfamiliar genres because my ethnicity has not given me a chance to feel and analyse them. The liking may only get developed later on after enough exposure to a foreign music. But it also depends on my previous training and experience.

Ethnicity itself involves social factors which can affect the process of development of aesthetics. A popular anecdote often discussed is from 1971 when Pandit Ravi Shankar and Ustad Ali Akbar Khan received applause from a naive western audience at a concert in New York when they had just finished tuning their instruments.

As far as the economy is concerned, it is a silent factor which turns and directs the nature and aesthetics of a person and contributes to his overall personality, too. The 'rich' or 'poor' status of a person and his family along with surroundings and belongings mostly makes a difference to his taste. This difference could be disastrous or fruitful, depending on the conditions.

CHAPTER 6

AESTHETICS OF CHORDS
IN INDIAN FILM MUSIC

"Indian film sound had little impact on orchestral music till around 1948. After that, harmonic effects came into picture because there was an influence of Portuguese music and all the arrangers and musicians were from Goa. There were a lot of harmonies, three-part harmony, it came after 1950. The then music directors also wanted a fresh sound. They started to get influenced by western films. So, the scenario changed. Before that the orchestra used to play in unison only. The concept of string section was not in its original form. After the arrangers from Goa came, the sound changed because they were real composers. They started to use different harmonies, and obbligatos.

-Merlin D'souza

AESTHETICS OF CHORDS IN INDIAN FILM MUSIC

As far as aesthetics of Indian Film Music regarding chords and orchestration is concerned, conclusively Indian film music is a form of art of its own kind. It has developed its own traditions which are being followed for generations. The development of this tradition has been achieved in a very short time. It has its own aesthetics which are contributed by different cultures and traditions of India as well as worldwide music.

Indian film music is currently the perfect blend of different music styles of India and the world. Almost every sound style and genre has been adapted by Indian film music in a very successful way.

The aesthetics always involves interpretive psycho-neuro-analysis and its conversion into musical structures. Aesthetics of film music involves the choice of listener, trends and patterns for the particular situation etc. Both listener and composer don't have full control on them in aesthetic assumptions. It's not an isolated phenomenon. Empathy is a decisive factor which helps attain a specific level of aesthetic sense.

Be it film music or any other music, the thought process of making a tune is almost the same, as far as my opinion is concerned. This process involves steps like perception-building, making a theme, developing a theme to a musical structure, reaching a perfect tune, testing for acceptance and presentation design of a tune. As far as chords are concerned, the knowledge of chords entirely affects the tunemaking positively. Sometimes, the root note of a composition and its tonic chord may be different because of the style of progression of notes. We can call it a change of *"chalan"* (a peculiar tendency of using notes in a certain way) in reference to Indian classical music. In Indian music, there are many *ragas*; if compared with the western scale and chord progression system, they do have different root notes, like in the case when C is a root note and tonic chord is A_b, as it sometimes happens with the composition of Bhairavi *raga*.

So, it is all about aesthetics which always is a decisive factor for a tune. Indian film music has its own aesthetic values which have developed over time. Because of the effect and blend of different musical styles of the world, Indian film music has a vibrant, unique character. This is the result of openness and acceptance towards world music culture.

Indian film music, since the time of its inception, was fond of the Parsi theatre music style and it still is to some extent. The same is the case with all the styles accepted in the course of development. In Indian film music, the *raga* system and chord systems are used individually or even simultaneously for tunemaking. Both the systems are well used and given importance. While working with both systems, we may get a good blend of *raga* color with accidentals based on its progression. Both these procedures have been used in film music: making a tune with a *raga* and implying chord progression inputs, or making a tune on a progression and implying the shadow of a *raga*. The knowledge of Indian ragas and different chord progressions and ability to make fruitful experiments provides better chances to make a more acceptable and prettier tune. It is all about where the aesthetics of the composer gets involved with a good understanding of the beauty of chords and harmonies; indefinite patterns of melodies may be created in many different ways.

As the orchestra grew in size in the Indian film music, the orchestration techniques got incorporated in aspects of harmony and chord. Previously, the songs were based on melodic movements of a *raga*, the songs later came in picture with a blend of chord progressions and harmonies.

In the initial stage, the orchestra was used as just a melodic accompaniment. Later on, the harmonic movements got importance in the part of orchestration. Mostly, the music contains use of major and minor triads only with a very rare use of seventh, diminished, suspended and sometimes sixth. Since the mid 1990s, when electronic and computerized music got a boom, an adaptation of complex harmonies and chords has been seen widely in Indian film music. It happened because music composers got busy in arrangements, too, with the hi-tech computerised sound recording modules. Although the arpeggios, resonators etc. got introduced in film music from the mid-1970s, they became popular only by the mid-1990s.

In film music, music arrangers and assistants have played a vital role since the beginning. The arrangers earlier held the key position for making the final picture of aesthetics of a composer. These arrangers usually hailed from Goa, and had an expertise in western music along with an aptitude of Indian music. Some of the most successful arrangers were Sebastian D'Souza, Johnny Gomes, Anthony Gonsalves, Chic Chocolate, Chris Parry, Amar Haldipur, Jaikumar Parte aka Baal Parte, Basu Chakroborthy, Kishore Sharma, Anil Mohile, Uttam Singh, Manohari Singh, and Master Sonik who actually contributed towards developing the individuality of their music composers with their sound and perfect orchestration patterns.

Generally, in Indian film music, producers and directors of films describe the situation to a music composer for which the song has to be composed. The briefing made is inclusive of genre, style (like *mujra*, outdoor romantic song, club song etc), the artist going to act on the song, story, character etc. The composer goes with the theme of the song and makes an emotional sensible base according to his feels, experiences and aesthetics expertise. After that he conceptualises the basic musical structure, with an eye and view regarding rhythm, keynote, progression, orchestration etc. He also keeps harmonisation, reharmonisation, and singing patterns in his mind during this creative process. This melodic structure is referred to as the perfect tune. This perfect tune then goes into discussion with the crew of the film. After discussion, the tune is finalised along with some creative inputs (if possible and present) and approved for designing of presentation that is called design of sound track which finally gets concluded by sound programming, acoustic dubbing (musical, vocal, chorus), final mixing and mastering of the track for appropriate media like cinema hall, CD, FM radio etc.

Chords and harmonies are the subject of proper training. By knowledge and proper training, they get attached to the thought process of the composer. Arnold Schoenberg advised that composers have to be conscious of harmony while making a melody. Both melody and harmony are interdependent and have a strong relation.

The aesthetics of a chord is a character to find the maximised competence and suitability of a chord for a particular part of melody or phrase. This character depends on the knowledge and experience. The composer has to be experienced about all kinds of sounds so that he can predict the level of acceptance or rejection of a particular sound whether it is a chord, phrase, timbre, style or anything else in the aspect of composition. Aesthetics of chords is just like the aesthetics of speech. How our brain decides the word to express the right meaning, the same process occurs when we work on chords. It is a matter of choice as well as data of the related subject stored in our memory.

Individuality of the composer is a decisive factor, that he chooses any particular chord. However, choices come to mind as chord and its inversion, extension, alteration, substitution, accidentals, chromatic changes etc. This is all how the aesthetics of chords works and comes into existence.

The aesthetics of chords doesn't give a final verdict for an expression, but it develops and enhances the imagination of the mood and emotion in a sharper way. This aesthetic sense works to reduce the difference between things experienced and things imagined. Also, this aesthetic sense works for bonding properties which makes relation between audience and composer to perceive a mood or emotion. Everything related to imagination, originated by the music, is dependent on the prior experience of composer and listener.

As far as film music or any music is concerned, form of harmony is a facilitator which contributes as the contrast of thoughts or emotions with the help of chords. Chord progression and its orchestral distribution aims towards the enhancement of expression of mood and emotion. Though any chord, in isolation, is not expressive (in terms of mood), but when it comes in composition through a chord progression, then it certainly reflects the expression. The distribution of notes of chords in orchestration is also a deciding factor regarding the emotion and expression.

The progression of chords is rather more expressive as the factor of enhancement of moods. In any key signature, every flat and sharp note also gives an impact in terms of expression, as Sir James Jeans discussed in the book *'Science and Music'*. To make a song beautiful, with a nice melody, all the musical elements related to presentation like playing, voicing, harmonisation along with the usage of chords, modes, scales and progressions are the responsible factors associated with aesthetics.

Here are some suggestions to get aesthetics developed towards chords and their usage during the process of tune or melody making and orchestration especially in context of light and film music production in India.

1. A composer must get the deepest knowledge about the lyrics, situation, location, actor, story, character etc., for which the music is being composed.
2. The composer must be aware of media for which the tune is being composed.
3. The composer must get clearer references regarding situation, style etc.
4. The composer must get the knowledge about timbre and peculiarities of the instruments. Timbre suggests the right placing of the key for the particular instrument.
5. The division of harmonies in different octaves must be done carefully and correctly so that the composer can achieve the desired result in context of beauty and emotional expression.
6. Different instruments sound better in some specific playing styles. This knowledge gives better results regarding aesthetic values.
7. A composer must have good knowledge, and experience of chords, harmonies and their usages.
8. Experimentation and openness towards usage of chords, harmonies and progressions gives better drive for best tune and its orchestration.
9. A composer must have good working conditions to make good tunes.
10. A composer should have a good capacity of making the transitions of moods to reach at the desired mental status for a tune.
11. A composer must have the capacity of controlled and planned imaginations for a particular mood or situation.

12. A composer should have the ability to create correlation of senses, experience and interpretation.
13. A composer should possess a good level of observation, supervision, survey and analysis skills of musical elements so that a better musical planning can be done.

A composer must have a good capacity of experimentation to get pleasant variations in chords with the help of addition, substitution, extension, chromatic alteration etc.

BIBLIOGRAPHY

1. Morcom, Anna. *Hindi Film Songs and the Cinema.* Ashgate Publishing Limited, 2007.
2. Jeans, James. *Science and Music.* Cambridge University Press, 1961.
3. Schoenberg, Arnold. *Fundamentals of Music Composition.* Edited By Gerald Strang and Leonard Stein, London, Boston: Faber and Faber, 1967.
4. Schoenberg, Arnold. *Structural Functions of Harmony.* London, Boston: Faber & Faber
5. Benson, Bruce Ellis. *The Improvisation of Musical Dialogue, A Phenomenology of Music.* Cambridge University Press, 2003 (preface).
6. Dutton, Denis. *Aesthetic Universals, The Routledge Companion to aesthetics.* Edited by Berys Gaut and dominic McIver Lopes, London And New York: Routledge Taylor & Francis Group, 2005
7. Vajpayi, Dr. Rajendra. *Saundarya.* Bhopal: Madhya Pradesh Hindi Granth Academy, 2009
8. Graham, Gordon. *Philosophy of The Arts, An Introduction to Aesthetics.* Third Edition, London And New York: Routledge, Taylor and Francis Group, 2005
9. Vimal, Dr. Kumar. *Saundarya Shastra Ke Tattva.* 5th edition, New Delhi: Rajkamal Prakashan,1989
10. Vanderberg, Kyle. *Aesthetics of Music, Good Enough: The Young Composer And The Search For Aesthetics.* 2009, publication N.A.
11. Livio, Mario. *The Golden Ratio.* New York, Broadway Books, date - N.A., publication N.A.
12. Korsakov, Nicolas Rimsky. *Principles of Orchestration.* edited by Maximilian Steinberg, English translation by Edward Agate, New York, London: E.F. Kalmus orchestra scores, Inc. date N.A.
13. Sanyal, Ritwik. *Philosophy of Music.* p. 206 as quotes by Anjali Mittal in "Hindustani Music" and The Aesthetic Concept and Form, New Delhi: D.K. Printworld (P) LTD, 2000
14. Miller, Ron. *Modal Jazz Composition and Harmony.* vol.2, date - N.A., publication N.A.
15. Adler, Samuel. *The Study of Orchestration.* Second edition, New York, London: W.W.Norton and Company Inc., 1989

16. Acharya, Sharmistha. *Bollywood and Globalization.* Thesis Submitted to San Francisco State University.
17. Zuckerkandl, Victor. *Sound and Symbol.* Pantheon Books, 1956 (as quoted by Dr. Kumar Vimal in Saundarya Shastra Ke Tattva, Rajkamal Prakashan, New Delhi, 5th ed. 1981)
18. Piston, Walter. *Orchestration.* London: Victor Gollancz Ltd. 1969
19. Margolis, Joseph. *Medieval Aesthetics, The Routledge Companion To Aesthetics,* Edited By Berys Gaut and Dominic Mc Iver Lopes, London , New York: Routledge, Taylor & Francis Group, 2005
20. Wilkins, Margaret Lucy. *Creative Music Composition, The Young Composers*
21. Voice, New York, London: Routledge, Taylor and Francis Group, 2006
22. Megh, Ramesh Kuntal. *Athato Saundarya Jigyasa,* New Delhi. Vani Prakashan, 2001

ARTICLES/WEB LINKS/INTERVIEWS

1. Hofmann-Engl, Ludger. Virtual Pitch and the Classification of Chords in Minor and Major Keys. Retrieved from: http://www.chameleongroup.org.uk/research/ICMPC_10.pdf
2. Liebman, David. A Chromatic Approach to Jazz Harmony and Melody, as appeared in google search on sept 2014, Publication N.A., date N.A.
3. Belkin, Alan, Artistic Orchestration, 2001, retrieved from www.dolmetsch.com/O.pdf
4. Aesthetics, Dynamics and Musical Scales: A golden connect, July an H.E. Cartwright, Diego L. Gonzalez, Oreste Piro & Domanico Stanzial, Published in J. New Music Research 31, 51-58, 2002. Retrieved from google.co.in search engine on 09/11/13.
5. Chords - The Source in History and Physics. Retrieved from http://fiddleguru.com/subscribers/chords.html as appeared on 02/08/2014
6. Berndt, Axel Berndt; Theisel, Holger Theisel. Adaptive Musical Expression from Automatic Realtime Orchestration and Performances. Retrieved from: http://wwwpub.zih.tu-dresden.de/~aberndt/publications/ICIDS08-2.pdf as appeared in google search on Sept. 2014
7. Herbert M. Schueller, Immanuel Kant and the Aesthetics of Music, The Journal of Aesthetics and Art Criticism, Vol.14, No.2, Second Special Issue on Baroque style in Various Arts. (Dec. 1955) pp. 218-247, retrieved from www.Jstor.org as appeared on 18/11/2008 16:35:51.

8. Wright, Howard. FAQ: The Guide To Chord Theory.. Retrieved from: www.museweb.com/ag/chord_form.html
9. Music Theory: Scales. Retrieved from: www.lotusmusic.com/lm_scales.html on 09/11/2013.
10. Pete Thomas, http://www.petethomas.co.uk/composition-arranging/definitions.html(2de2)[2003/03/17 23:29:45]
11. The Elements of Music, Which.edu/mus-gened/mus 150/ ch-1 elements.pdf, page-4.
12. The Physics of Sound - The Method behind the music, http://method-behind-the-music.com/mehanics/physics as appeared on 02/08/2014. page-1

FUNDAMENTAL BOOKS

1. The Routledge Companion to Aesthetics. Edited by Berys Gaut and Dominic McIver Lopes
2. Listening Through the Noise - The Aesthetics of Experimental Electronic Music: Joanna Demers. (Oxford University Press, 2010)
3. The Cognitive Processing of Film and Musical Soundtracks: Marilyn G Boltz. (Haverford College, Haverford, Pennsylvania)
4. The Study of Orchestration. Samuel Adler. (W. W. Norton and Company)
5. Structural Functions of Harmony – Arnold Schoenberg (Publisher- Faber and Faber- London- Boston)
6. The Improvisation of Musical Dialogue - A Phenomenology of Music- bruce ellis benson (Cambridge University Press)
7. An Introduction to Kant's Aesthetics - Core Concepts and Problems: Christian Helmut Wenzel (Blackwell Publishing)
8. Classic and Romantic German Aesthetics: J. M. Bernstein. (Cambridge University Press)
9. Conventional Wisdom-The Content of Musical Form: Susan McClary (University of California Press)
10. Creative Music Composition-The Young Composer's Voice- Margaret Lucy Wilkins (Routldge- Tayler & Francis Group)
11. Sweet Anticipation-Music and the Psychology of Expectation: David Huron. (The MIT Press Cambridge)
12. The Principles of Aesthetics: Dewitt H Parker
13. Fundamentals of Musical Compositions: Arnold Schoenberg- (Faber and Faber)
14. The Larger forms of Musical Composition: Percy Goetschius (G. Schirmer. Inc)
15. Hegel's Aesthetics- A Critical Exposition: By John Steixfokt Kedxey. (S. C. Griggs And Company)

16. Directing Film Techniques And Aesthetics: Michael Rabiger. (Focal Press)
17. Music, Language, and Cognition and Other Essays in the Aesthetics of Music: Peter Kivy. (Clarendon Press)
18. The Cognition of Basic Musical Structures-David Temperley (The MIT Press Cambridge)
19. Musical Creativity-Multidisciplinary Research in Theory and Practice-Edited by Irène Deliège and Geraint A. Wiggins- (Psychology Press)
20. Philosophy Of The Arts-An Introduction to Aesthetics: Gordon Graham-(Routledge)
21. Mystic Chords-Mysticism and Psychology in Popular Music- Manish Soni (Algora Publishing New York)
22. The Physics Of Music And Musical Instruments: David R. Lapp
23. Music Composition- *Michael Miller* (ALPHA A member of Penguin Group (USA) Inc.)
24. Orchestration – Walter Piston (Victor Gollancz Ltd)
25. Hindustani Music and the Aesthetic Concept of Form- Anjali Mittal. (D. K. Printworld Pvt Ltd, New Delhi)
26. Theory of Indian Music- Rai Bahadur Bishan Swarup. (Pilgrims Publishing, Varanasi)
27. Language of Music: V. K. Narayana Menon. (Publications Division, Ministry of Information & Broadcasting, Government of India)
28. Paashchatya Swarlipi Paddhati Evam Bhartiya Sangeet- Dr. Swatantra Sharma- Pratibha Prakashan Delhi
29. Athaato Saundarya Jigyasa- Ramesh Kuntal Megh. (Vani Prakashan)
30. Lalitya Tatwa: Hajari Prasad Dwivedi. (Vani Prakashan)
31. Saundarya Tatwa Nirupan: S. C. Narsinghachari (Rajkamal Prakashan)
32. Sakshi Hai Saundarya Prashnik- Ramesh Kuntal Megh (Rajkamal Prakashan)
33. Saundarya Shashtra Ke Tatwa- Kumar Vimal. (Rajkamal Prakashan)
34. Sadharnikaran Aur Saundaryanubhuti- Dr. Premkant Tandon. (Lokbharti Prakashan)
35. Film Ka Saundarya Shashtra Aur Bhartiya Cinema: Kamla Prasad. (Shilpayan)

REFERENCE BOOKS

1. Generalized Musical Intervals and Transformations-David Lewin- (Oxford University Press) 2007
2. A Chromatic Approach to Jazz and Harmony: David Leibman

3. A Dictionary of Musical Terms: Dr. T. H. Baker
4. Knowing Art - Essays in Aesthetics and Epistemology: Edited by Matthew Kieran and Dominic Mciver Lopes
5. Lectures on Musical Life: William Sterndale Bennett (The Boydell)
6. The Equation That Couldn't Be Solved-How Mathematical Genius Discovered the Language of Symmetry: Mario Livio. (Simon & Schuster Paperbacks)
7. The Technique of my Musical Language: Olivier Messiaen- (Alphanse Leduc- Paris) 1944)
8. Music That Works - Contributions of Biology, Neurophysiology, Psychology, Sociology, Medicine and Musicology. Edited by Roland Haas, Vera Brandes (Springer Wien, New York)
9. Musical Knowledge-Intuition, Analysis and Music Education- Keith Swanwick- (Routledge)
10. Musical Meaning-Toward a Critical History-Lawrence Kramer- (University of California Press)
11. Musical Symbolism in the Operas of Debussy and Bartók: Trauma, Gender, and the Unfolding of the Unconscious: Elliott Antokoletz (Oxford University Press)
12. Listening to the Sirens- Musical Technologies of Queer Identity from Homer to *Hedwig*-Judith A. Peraino (University Of California Press)
13. Romanticism, Aesthetics, And Nationalism- David Aram Kaiser (Cambridge University Press)
14. Singing in Musical Theatre - The Training of Singers and Actors- Joan Melton (Allworth Press)
15. Such Freedom, If Only Musical - Unofficial Soviet Music During The Thaw: Peter J. Schmelz (Oxford University Press)
16. The Biology of Musical Performance and Performance-Related Injury- Alan H. D. Watson (The Scarecrow Press, Inc.)
17. The Continental Aesthetics Reader: Edited by Clive Cazeaux (Routledge)
18. The Golden Ratio - The Story of Phi, the World's Most Astonishing Number: Mario Livio (Broadway Books)

Articles

1. Aesthetics, Dynamics, And Musical Scales: A Golden Connection: Julyan H. E. Cartwright_, Diego L. Gonz´alezyz, Oreste Pirox, & Domenico Stanzialy. Published in J. New Music Research 31, 51–58, 2002)
2. A Graphical Model for Chord Progressions Embedded in a Psychoacoustic Space: Jean-Fran»cois. (University of Montreal)

3. A Pregroup Grammar For Chord Sequences - Richard G. Terrat
4. Cross-Cultural Perception & Structure of Music-William H. Jackson, 1998. *Organizational Learning & Instructional Technologies.* University of New Mexico,
5. Psychology in Music: the Rôle of Experimental Psychology in the Science and Art of Music -Author(s): C. E. Seashore Source: The Musical Quarterly, Vol. 16, No. 2 (Apr., 1930), pp. 229-237 Published by: Oxford University Press Stable URL: http://www.jstor.org/stable/738449
6. The Process of Musical Creation- The Current State of Research: Federico Garcia
7. The Cognitive Processing of Film and Musical Soundtracks: Marilyn G. Boltz (Haverford College, Haverford, Pennsylvania)
8. Vision Of Equinox For Orchestra: Maiko Chiba. (School of Music)

IMAGES

1. Courtesy- Sharda Rajan
2. Copyright@Abhishek Tripathi
3. Courtesy- Sunil Kaushik
4. Courtesy- Merlin D'souza
5. Courtesy- Shridhar Nagraj